COLLINS GEM

BUILDINGS

OF

BRITAIN

Patricia & Bruce Robertson
with
The Diagram Group

D1313081

HarperCollins*Publishers*

HarperCollins Publishers
P.O. Box, Glasgow G4 0NB

A Diagram Book first created by Diagram Visual
Information Limited of 195 Kentish Town Road,
London NW5 8SY, England

First published 1992
© Diagram Visual Information Limited 1992
Reprint 10 9 8 7 6 5 4 3 2 1 0

ISBN 0 00 458975 0

Printed in Great Britain by
HarperCollins Manufacturing, Glasgow

Introduction

"It will be readily admitted that the great test of architectural beauty is the fitness of the design to the purpose for which it is intended, and that the style of a building should so correspond with its use that the spectator may at once perceive the purpose for which it is erected."

A.W.N. Pugin 1812–52
Victorian architect

Understanding the reasons for the construction of a building helps you enjoy the experience of exploring it. Each building reveals clues to its historical, architectural and cultural origins in the materials used, the style and detail of its features, and its relationship to surrounding buildings.

The buildings in this book are arranged into seven groups: Domestic, Religious, Military and military-style, Public, Agricultural, Industrial and Monuments and follies.

Domestic. Domestic architecture stands as evidence of the social history of Britain. The house we live in says a great deal about the life-style of the first occupants. A duke's ancestral home or a 20th-century housing estate reflect the social conditions at the time when they were built.

Religious. Those buildings used for generations in the worship of God have become monuments to the nation's cultural heritage. The 1,500 years of Christian church building have produced styles whose names are now used to classify periods of British architecture.

Military and military-style. Throughout 4,000 years neighbours or invaders have fought for control of these islands. The victors built castles and fortifications to protect their possessions, and those after the retreat of the Romans provide a history of the British monarchy.

Public. Wherever groups of people gathered together for mutual benefit, the buildings they occupied were as grand as they could afford. Town halls, schools, colleges, museums, stadia, theatres, inns and hotels have gradually changed in style, usually in response to the changing needs of the community.

Agricultural. Almost always functional, many farm buildings are now obsolete as the early methods of farming have been replaced by new techniques.

Industrial. During the later part of the 18th century new industrial needs required new types of buildings. Custom-built structures now often stand derelict as newer industries disregard the previous generations' solutions in favour of new materials and environments.

Monuments and follies. Monuments are buildings constructed to commemorate events or the deceased. Follies are usually works built to satisfy the eccentric fancies of their patrons. With little or no functional purpose, monuments and follies allow their designers a greater degree of creative freedom.

Contents

Major Periods of British Architecture

12000 – 3000 BC	Mesolithic Age (middle stone age)
3000 – 1800 BC	Neolithic Age (new stone age)
1800 – 550 BC	Bronze Age
550 – AD 43	Iron Age
43 – 400	Roman
400 – 650	Dark Ages
650 – 1066	Anglo-Saxon
1066 – 1189	Norman
1189 – 1307	Early English
1307 – 1350	Decorated
1327 – 1520	Perpendicular
1520 – 1558	Tudor
1558 – 1603	Elizabethan
1603 – 1625	Jacobean
1625 – 1689	Stuart
1689 – 1720	Queen Anne (Baroque)
1720 – 1830	Georgian
1810 – 1830	Regency (Late Georgian)
1837 – 1901	Victorian
1901 – 1914	Edwardian
1922 to date	International Style (Modern)

Major British architectural styles explained

Anglo-Saxon. Most early buildings were of wood and have disappeared. Stone churches survive in a simplified round-arched style.

Art Deco. A 1920s to 1930s style, characterized by geometrical shapes, stylized natural forms, and symmetrical designs.

Art Nouveau. From the 1880s to 1910 architects such

as Charles Rennie Mackintosh adapted sinuous natural forms which were applied to *objets d'art*, costumes, and the shapes of windows, doors and mouldings.

Arts and Crafts. A 19th-century style of design inspired by, and applied to, everyday objects; it stressed medieval skills, in reaction to industrialism.

Baroque. A European style, confined to churches and palaces, in which Classical forms and motifs were transformed by inventive use of space and decorations.

Classical. Plans, details and facades based upon Greco-Roman styles. Common from the 16th century to today.

Decorated. Second phase of the English Gothic style.

Early English. The development from Norman architecture in which the preceding techniques were refined to produce the first Gothic elements.

Elizabethan. The Renaissance style as introduced and developed during the reign of Elizabeth I.

Georgian. The British refinement of the Renaissance ideals, which itself had adapted Classical criteria. It was prevalent during the reigns of the Georges.

Gothic. Originated in Europe and thrived from the late 12th to the early 16th centuries. Most expressive in churches, it was characterized by pointed arches.

Gothic Revival. A 19th-century attempt to apply the ornament and aspirations of the Gothic architects.

Greek Revival. A competitor to the Gothic revival. It was the 18th and 19th centuries' way of creating buildings echoing the simple purity of Greek temples.

International Style. Influenced by the German Bauhaus school of architecture, it was characterized by undecorated rectangular forms, typified by high-rise buildings.

Jacobean. Named after James I, it was the flowering of the Elizabethan Renaissance style. It featured Classical details grafted onto medieval-style buildings.

Modern. Many modern buildings are based on the Bauhaus-derived International Style.

Neo-Classical. An 18th- and 19th-century Classical style with heavy emphasis on achieving a balance of simple shapes and masses.

Norman. The British Romanesque style introduced from Normandy after the conquest of 1066.

Perpendicular. The final phase in British Gothic architecture. Engineering efficiency in stone building techniques produced increasingly refined structures.

Queen Anne. See Baroque. This style also featured skilled brickwork in domestic architecture.

Regency. Like Neo-Classicism, this was a Classical style normally characterized by a restrained simplicity.

Renaissance. In British architecture this refers to the rediscovery of ancient Classical forms and building details from the early 16th to the early 19th centuries.

Stuart. Largely domestic architecture with semi-Classical form and Dutch influences.

Transitional. Those buildings containing earlier Norman elements, but developing towards the Gothic.

Tudor. The transition of Gothic to Renaissance during the reign of Henry VII.

Victorian. Architecture partly associated with the Gothic revival but also incorporating much later Classical work. It was often based on Italian and French architecture and sometimes featured the use of cast iron. The term is applied to architecture constructed during the reign of Queen Victoria.

The following seven pages group the buildings in this book according to historical period.

Pre-Roman

Domestic	33, 40, 42–43, 48–49
Religious	70–71
Military	108–109
Agricultural	182–183
Monuments	234

Broch, Mousa, Shetland, 4th to 2nd century BC.

Roman and Saxon

Domestic	33, 52–53
Religious	72–73, 82–83
Military	110–113
Public	164
Agricultural	183–184, 197
Industrial	220
Monuments	240–241

Saxon Chapel, Bradford-on-Avon, Warwickshire, 7th century AD.

Norman and Early English: 1066–1307

Domestic	34–35, 54–55
Religious	84–91, 106–107
Military	112–113, 116–123
Public	170
Agricultural	185
Monuments	240–243

Durham Cathedral, Co. Durham, 1093–1133. The finest Norman cathedral in Britain.

Decorated and Perpendicular: 1307–1520

Cruck House, Didbrook, Gloucestershire.

Early Renaissance: 1520–1603

Little Moreton Hall, Cheshire, 1559.

Late Renaissance and Georgian: 1603–1810

Mereworth Castle, Kent, 1722. Based very closely on the Villa Capra near Venice, Italy, designed by Antonio Palladio in the 16th century.

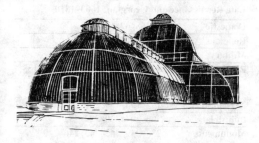

Palm House, Kew Gardens, London, 1844–8.
Decimus Burton's wrought-iron symbol of Victorian
architectural and engineering virtuosity.

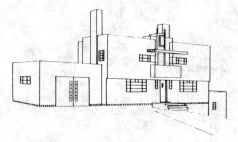

Detached House, Braintree, Essex, 1925. An early
example of the International Style in Britain.

19th Century: 1810–1900

Gatwick Airport, Surrey, 1958.

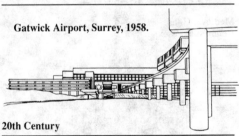

20th Century

The following eight pages group the buildings in this book according to the regions in which they occur.

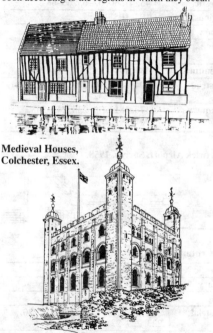

**Medieval Houses,
Colchester, Essex.**

The White Tower, The Tower of London, 1086–97.

South East and East Anglia

Domestic	36–37, 41, 45, 47, 58, 64, 66–68
Religious	80, 83, 86, 99, 104
Military	113, 118–119, 124, 132–133
Public	136–137, 146–147, 149, 152, 154–155, 158–160, 162–163, 168, 170, 174–175, 179–180
Agricultural	189, 191, 193, 198–200, 202–203
Industrial	204–205, 215, 220, 231–232
Monuments	237, 240–245, 248

London and Home Counties

Domestic	45, 52–53, 56, 61, 65–67
Religious	81, 87, 99–105
Military	130, 134
Public	138, 141–147, 149–150, 153, 155–164, 166–167, 169, 171–175, 177–178, 180–181
Agricultural	192–193
Industrial	205, 208–211, 214–215, 218, 224–233
Monuments	235–239, 242–244, 246

Pulteney Bridge, Bath, Avon, 1770.

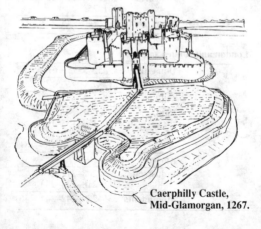

**Caerphilly Castle,
Mid-Glamorgan, 1267.**

South and South West

Domestic	32–33, 40–42, 47, 53, 63, 67
Religious	70–71, 90–91
Military	108, 112–113
Public	144, 172, 180
Agricultural	182–184, 188–189, 197
Industrial	212–213, 220–221, 223, 225, 226–228
Monuments	234, 238, 240–241

Farmhouse, Dartmoor, 17th century.

Wales

Domestic	43, 63–64, 50
Military	120–123
Public	164
Agricultural	186, 198
Industrial	208
Monuments	245, 247

Bottle Kilns, Etruria, Staffordshire, 1769.

Gaythorn Hall, Cumbria, 17th century.

Midlands

Domestic	32–35, 54–59, 62, 67, 69
Religious	81, 83, 87, 95, 104–105
Public	152–153, 165, 170–171, 176
Agricultural	192
Industrial	206–207, 209–210, 222, 224–225, 228
Monuments	240–241, 244–246

North

Domestic	37, 59–60, 65
Religious	82–83, 90–91, 95, 103, 106–107
Military	110–111, 125
Public	139–140, 144, 146–147, 150–151, 165, 168–169, 174–175, 179
Agricultural	183, 185, 187, 194–197, 201
Industrial	206–207, 216–217, 219, 233
Monuments	239–241, 248–249

Eilean Donan Castle, Inverness-shire, 1220. A
superbly restored castle, easily viewed from the
Lochalsh road to Skye.

**Cottage, Connemara, Co. Galway, Ireland, 18th
century.** A labourer's dwelling with a typical thatch
and rubble-walled construction.

Scotland

Domestic	43, 49–50
Religious	73, 104
Military	109–110, 125–133
Public	138–139, 151, 156–157, 160, 181
Industrial	204, 210–211, 213, 219
Monuments	234, 236, 246–247, 249

Ireland

Domestic	43, 49, 68
Religious	72–73
Public	148
Agricultural	197

1. Domestic Buildings

Modern buildings, as well as great houses and public buildings of the past, were shaped primarily by taste, culture and needs.

The construction of smaller, humbler dwellings in Britain was for 2,000 years the result of locally available materials, primitive technology and weather conditions. The six maps on the following pages show the distribution of the main types of building material. These materials enable us to assess approximately the type of early simple building found in these areas.

1. Sandstone. Has a variety of weather repellent qualities. Softer sandstones were used for wall construction with the stronger grey sandstone or granite for corners or dressing windows. It is available in southern Ireland, Scotland, Wales and throughout England.

2. Limestone. Is found in an area forming a diagonal band extending from Dorset to Yorkshire, and also in much of Ireland. The stone is easy to work, so large slabs can be dressed to make roofing slates or cut to individual sizes in the construction of irregular walls.

3. Granite. Undressed granite was used for local building of small houses which occur in Cornwall and Wales and coastal areas of Ireland. When worked into blocks it was mostly used to construct corners or windows and door surrounds.

4. Chalks and Flint. Chalk is not used directly as a building material, but when burnt it makes lime for plaster. Within chalk beds are deposits of flint, small and very hard stones which can be set into walls as construction material or as decoration. The location is almost entirely in the south east of England.

5. Stones and Random Rubble. Usually found on upland and moorland districts from Wales to the Scottish Highlands. Also used for infilling in thick walls with a granite or sandstone face.

6. Brick. Where suitable clays are available bricks are the most common building material, which, as transportation systems improved, spread to all parts of Britain.

In addition to these basic mineral resources many small domestic houses were traditionally built of wood. Up to the 17th century there were many forests mainly containing hard woods which were used extensively for the construction and detailing of early buildings. In the 17th century the use of wood for iron smelting and ship-building, and the deforestation for the purpose of reclaiming land, seriously depleted the nation's timber resources.

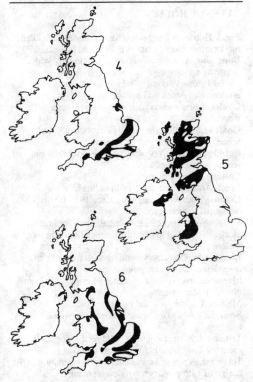

TYPES OF HOUSES

Black House. A long, single-storey, dry-stone walled, turf or straw-roofed cottage in Scotland or Ireland.

Bungalow. A one-storey house. Traditionally with overhanging eaves.

Bastel House. A home in which the residential quarters are above livestock and storage space.

Chalet. Swiss-style cottage or bungalow made of wood.

Chateau. French-style, usually decorative, grand house.

Cobbled House. Consisting of dry-stone walls and roofed with a domed top.

Cottage. A small house.

Croft. Another term for "smallholding".

Council House. Housing built since 1919 funded by municipal authorities.

Lodge. Not necessarily residential, often for hunting parties. Now used to describe the gate house on an estate.

Longhouse. One-storey building with residents and livestock under one continuous roof.

Manor House. Usually of medieval origins, the home of a local landowner.

Manse. A home provided for clergy.

Semi-detached. Two houses joined to form one building.

Tenement. A large house or building divided into rooms or flats, usually for separate rental.

Terraced. A row of connected houses originating in the design of 18th-century town developments.

NAMES FOR PARTS OF A HOUSE

Atrium. The central courtyard of a Roman house.

Attic. The space between the roof and top-floor ceiling.

Basement. The lowest storey, frequently underground, and used as storage space or, in the 18th and 19th centuries, as servants' quarters.

Boudoir. A lady's changing room, usually at the side of a bedroom.

Buttery. A storage room for food and drink.

Chimney Breast. The protruding wall which contains the fireplace, hearth and flues.

Coal Cellar. Before central heating was invented houses were kept warm by burning coal which was usually stored in the basement or an outhouse.

Conservatory. Glass-panelled room, originally for growing subtropical and tropical plants.

Inglenook. A space at the side of an open fireplace, usually occupied by a bench or bed.

Larder. A room for storing food; essential before refrigerators were invented.

Loft. The room immediately under the roof.

Pantry. Like a larder, but also used for storing cooking utensils.

Parlour. A living room where guests were entertained in 19th-century houses.

Privy. Before sanitation improvements this was an outhouse used as a lavatory.

Scullery. A small kitchen, also used in working-class houses for the washing of clothes.

Solar. The upper room in a medieval house.

Vestibule. An entrance room or antechamber.

Early timber-framed houses did not survive the damp climate of the British Isles. Covered in turf or straw the roofs decomposed and collapsed. Only pot-holes survive as evidence of early house forms.

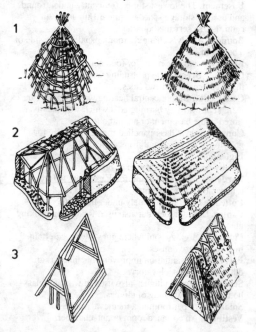

1. Early Hut Forms. None remain, but they were probably conical structures like wigwams, made from the widely available forest timbers.

2. Haldon, Devon. A Neolithic rectangular house. The side poles were set in a stone foundation and covered in a turf wall. The roof was probably turf.

3. Horncastle, Lincolnshire. This tent-like structure was introduced to Britain by the Saxons and Danes. The roof of thatch was kept in place by a net weighted with stones.

4

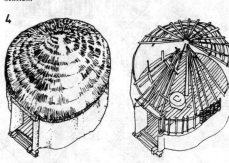

4. Glastonbury, Somerset. Large circular houses, built by Iron Age settlers in southern England. Groups of houses called "crannogs" were built on artificial islands of logs, peat and clay. Often as wide as 40 feet they had timber floors, clay and wattle walls and a huge log for centre support.

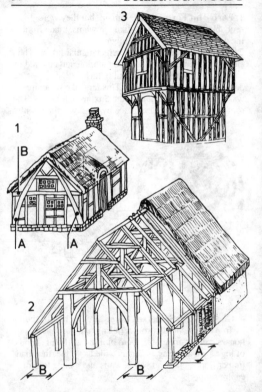

3

1

B

A   A

2

B   B   A

Three types of timber-framed houses developed in medieval times: the cruck house, the hall house with bays, and the box frame.

1. Cruck Houses. Large tree trunks were cut vertically down their length to make two equal-sized and shaped main supports or "crucks" (**A**). These were set at intervals with their narrow ends joined at the top. Tie beams (**B**) were placed across the two crucks to form the bases of the upper rooms and to hold the framework together.

Between pairs of crucks a ridge pole, side bars, wattle-woven walls and rafters were placed, which then provided a network onto which daubed clay (on the lower parts) and thatch (on the upper) could be hung.

2. Hall Houses. These were larger than cruck houses. They had a series of columned frames set at approximately 16-foot intervals. The bay (**A**) became the unit in which the size of the hall was measured. Normally 4 bays in length, the hall resembled a farm barn with an inner exposed roof structure and side aisles (**B**), which could be screened from the main hall with wattle partitions.

3. Box Frames: The Gatehouse, Lower Brockhampton, Herefordshire. This is a good, simple example of a box frame. During the later part of the Middle Ages large trees became more scarce, so box structures of smaller and shorter timbers became more popular. This method also allowed far more varied forms of building size and shape.

Central Hall Houses. During the Tudor period a larger farmhouse developed which had a central hall occupying the full height and width of the building, and two stories, set at right angles to it, at either end. Originally the hall would have had a communal hearth, and the lower side rooms for stores and cattle, while the upper side rooms would be sleeping chambers. As a result of their frequent location in the Weald of Kent these houses became known as Wealden houses.

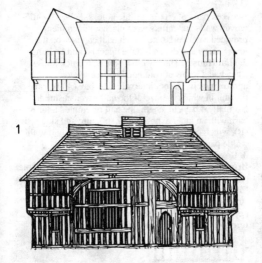

1

1. Link Farm, Egerton, Kent. An example of a central hall house built in the 16th century. It has one common roof, but still retains its side chambers and central hall. The narrow windowframes would have had thin, stretched animal skins over them as glass was too expensive for domestic use.

2. Morphany Hall, Runcorn, Cheshire. This detail of one section of the front shows the Tudor development of curved braces (**A**) and intermediate timbers (**B**). These have no structural value but were a feature of regional carpentry skills.

3. 20th-Century Tudor. The attractive appearance of darkened timber frames set out in contrasting white panels suggested to later architects the opportunity of decorating domestic dwellings. This house is made of brick, with the second-floor walls covered in thin, dark timbers (**A**) and a plaster-covered infill (**B**).

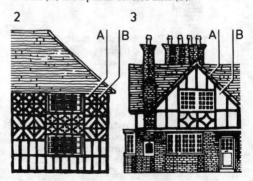

Timber-framed Houses. The early builders solved the problem of the infilling of the spaces between the vertical structural timbers and horizontal frame timbers by using any locally available material.

The infilling was often covered in plaster or painted, and in many cases the entire surface was plastered to protect the timbers and the edges between timber and infill.

Weather Boarding. Where timber was inexpensive, overlapping boards were horizontally fixed to the outside frame.

Panel Boarding. Interlocking vertical timbers provided another method in which shorter planks could be used.

Wattle and Daub. Vertically set wooden rods into which were woven thinner branches (the wattle) forming a rough basket-like surface, and over which plaster (the daub) was pressed.

Split Lath. Woven like wattle but made from slices of larger timbers.

Stone Infilling. Rubble, clay, straw and large stones could be built up into small panels.

Clay or Clay Lumps. Unlike clay-built houses which had thick walls and were irregular in shape, the timber-framed houses were able to support thin clay panels.

Brick. Set in small frames, the bricks were not load-bearing and formed no part of the structure of the house.

Brick Nogging. Set in diagonal patterns, these offered opportunities to vary the design of the wall surface.

There were three methods of building with unbaked clay. The first was to build it up with close-cropped thick turf sods. The second method (known as cob) was to take wet clay and mix it with chopped straw, gravel or small stones. The third (claybat) was to form the clay into slabs and build walls as if constructed from rough blocks.

All the methods required the external surface to be rendered to protect it from deterioration. A common method was to coat the surface regularly with a lime plaster and then to colour wash or tar the surface. Wet tar could have sand thrown at it, enabling the rough surface to be painted.

1. Early Pit Dwelling. None survive from the Iron Age. These would have been pits dug in clay soil, with the excavated earth being used to construct a surrounding wall, over which was built a timber roof covered in turf and bracken.

2. Ashton, Exeter, Devon. The tar band along the bottom is for protecting this cob building from the weather.

3. Branscombe, Seaton, Devon. Cob buildings were constructed gradually as the subsequent layers of clay dried out, so they tend to have a rounded and undulating appearance. Heavy buttresses were added on either side of the door to support the bulging walls.

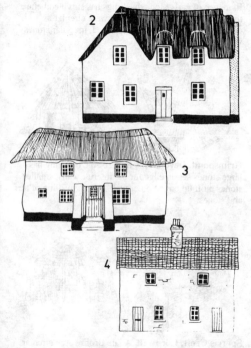

4. Shipham, Norfolk. Large sun-dried blocks (claybats) are laid in regular rows just like large bricks.

Evidence of early stone dwellings has survived better than those of wood. The earliest were circular as constructing corners from undressed, irregular stones was difficult.

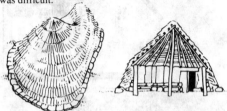

Grimspond, Devon. This Bronze Age dwelling has large stones set on edge for the interior walls, smaller stones built up on the outer wall, and an infilling of turf and stones.

Sperris Croft, Cornwall. A late Bronze Age circular house with stone walls built to shoulder height and a wood and turf roof.

Cobbled House. Dry-stone houses – without windows and possibly covered with turf – were built in the west of Ireland, Scotland, the Orkneys and Wales.

Black House, Arnol, Lewis, Scotland. A longhouse originally without windows, built with double walls of undressed stone, infilled with rubble, and containing a low-pitched roof of thatch, secured with straw ropes and stones.

1

The Celts were not able to fire bricks to the high temperature where they become permanently hard, so no Celtic brick buildings survive. Roman bricks, being thinner and larger than bricks today, were really tiles that were extremely well prepared and fired so that many still survive – although they may now appear incorporated in later buildings.

The Normans imported bricks but built their castles of stone. During the Middle Ages ships returning from selling wool in the low countries and Hanseatic ports returned with bricks for ballast. Traditional brick-makers worked from local sources, but by the 18th century brick manufacture had become an industry, and bricks were transported to all parts of the country.

Bricks have three structural benefits: they are fireproof, and so were used for chimneys; they are durable if kept dry; and their small size makes for an infinite variety of house shapes and sizes.

1. Manor Farm, St Neots, Cambridgeshire. A brick and clay tile building which contains window and door surrounds of plaster imitations of stone. Built about 1600, the Tudor chimneys show how bricks can be arranged to form complex structures.

2. Townhouse, King's Lynn, Norfolk, 1790. The use of brick had, by the 18th century, become extensive throughout Britain, and during the Georgian period simple brick facades were decorated with plaster or stone cornices, decorative metal balconies and painted wood surrounds to doors and windows.

3. 19th-Century Townhouse, No. 16 Bayham St, Camden Town, London. Once occupied by Charles Dickens's parents this is typical of thousands of cheaply built 19th-century brick houses. Terraces require only front and back double walls; the partitional walls between the houses can be thinner and they can share the structural weight of joint chimneys.

2

3

Flints occur in chalk strata where there is not usually any available building stone. Flints are small, hard and irregular, so the strength of a flint wall is in the binding mortar.

3

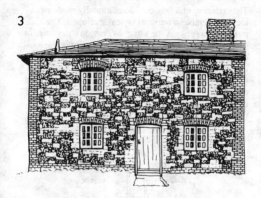

1. East Raynham, Norfolk. Most flint walls are
cornered or terminated by an interlocking brick column.
This protects the corners and prevents flints from
coming loose should they be exposed on more than one
side.

2. Cinder Hall, Little Walden, Essex. A dazzling
display of coloured flints, arranged in fleur-de-lis,
lozenges and squares. A distinctive work, with the
materials and colours arranged to form a unique facade
within a brick surround.

3. Upper Woodford, Wiltshire. Built in the mid-19th
century as a farm labourer's cottage. The strong
undressed stone slabs mingled with the flint make a
very durable wall surface, and the brick edgings provide
extra structural support.

The covering of a house was traditionally made from local materials, so regional styles developed. The purpose was always the same: to provide a dry interior (using the minimum weight), and to construct the most durable surface. Until new construction materials were introduced in the 20th century, it was always essential to build roofs with a sloping surface. Rain – and more damaging – snow must not stay on the roof, otherwise dampness penetrates into the inner structure and rots the frame and fabric of the house.

Turf. Used by Iron Age settlers to cover timber-framed round houses.

Cobbled Stone. Dry-stone structures, where the stones used for the construction of the walls become progressively smaller and thinner as they approach the apex of the circular house.

Soil and Twigs. A very early, primitive method of roof building was to weave a roof structure from twigs, strong enough to hold a layer of soil on which grew grass and foliage.

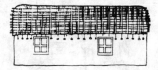

Heather. Thatched into thick layers tied down with weighted ropes, it was used on the Atlantic coasts of Ireland and Scotland.

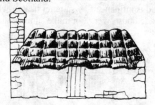

Straw and Reed. Light in weight and an excellent insulator. It required the special skills of the thatcher for its construction.

Sandstone. Scottish sandstone was often used for the roofs as well as the walls. Strong supporting walls were required for sandstone roofs.

Corrugated Iron. Sheets of thin iron often replaced previously thatched roofs, as the material was cheap and easy to use. This method was very unsatisfactory, as the metal is influenced by summer heat or winter frost. It made houses very hot in the summer and cold in the winter.

Pantiles. Originally imported by the Romans, the use of clay tiles formed by curved overlapping small panels is commonplace throughout the British Isles.

Asbestos. Until the discovery of respiratory damage caused by asbestos, 20th-century cottages were frequently covered in either decorative tiles or sheets of asbestos.

Limestone. This was often used if it was locally available, but like sandstone it required a strong supporting structure for its weight.

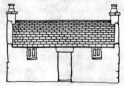

Slate. This is a graded slate roof, where the small slates appear nearer the ridge. 19th-century demand for Welsh slate tiles produced standard sizes and thicknesses for convenience.

1

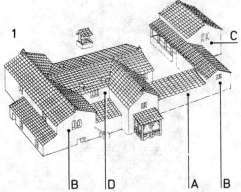

B   D   A   B

The Roman domestic buildings located in cities have
long since been replaced by newer structures, so very
little survives of their original construction. It is
assumed they were like those of the Mediterranean
region where the preserved remains of Pompeii gave an
indication of how a Romano-British townhouse might
have been laid out.

In the countryside the layout of villas has been more
easily deduced from surviving remains. The most usual
form of a Roman country house was a long building
with a corridor down one side, giving access to
individual rooms. These "corridor villas" seldom
survived in their original form, as increased rural
prosperity in the 400 years after the conquest resulted
in the building of additional rooms and cloisters.

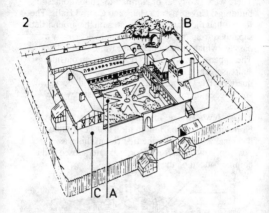

**1. Park Street Villa, Verulamium (St Albans),
Hertfordshire.** A 2nd-century villa with an original
corridor (**A**) with wings (**B**). In the 4th century the
wings were extended (**C**) and many of the central rooms
(**D**) rebuilt. Beyond the house would have been farm
buildings.

2. Villa, Chedworth, Gloucestershire. A 2nd-century
luxury villa with an enclosed garden (**A**), a wing for
servants and kitchens (**B**), and a granary and storehouse
(**C**). The buildings were of stone with timber used for
second-storey rooms and, amazingly, some windows
were of glass, almost 1,000 years before it came into use
again.

There were two types of Norman-to-Tudor domestic buildings: Cross Passage Halls and Central Halls. The former had the main gathering area on the ground floor, separated from the store, buttery and kitchens by a passage which crossed the house from front to back. The upper floor, which was reached by an outside staircase, was reserved for sleeping and private quarters. The Central Halls had a main hall occupying a space reaching up to the roof with two-storey side rooms.

1. The Jew's House, Lincoln. This is a rare surviving Norman townhouse. Built in the 1170s it would only have had a fireplace on the first floor. This was positioned over the front door, was later closed and a chimney added on the gabled end.

2. Haddon Hall, Derbyshire. A late-medieval house, begun in 1070 (the drawing shows its extent by 1624). The hall (**A**) is surrounded by two courtyards of service buildings: kitchens (**B**), pantry (**C**), buttery (**D**), aviary (**E**) and chapel (**F**).

3. Boothby Pagnell Manor House, Grantham, Lincolnshire. A Norman manor house. The upper floor was for the lord and guests. The lower ground floor would have been the hall and stores. At the time of building in 1200, entrance to the upper floor would have been by a wooden staircase. All of the windows were small. The large first-floor window in this view was added in later years.

Houses in the 16th century were often financed with the newly acquired wealth of the Tudor nouveaux-riches.

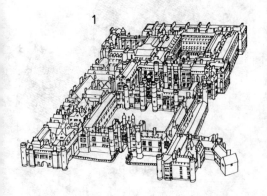

1. Hampton Court Palace, Greater London. Built from 1514 to 1540 (here shown as extended by Wren), it was originally the house of Cardinal Wolsey, who, as the head of the Church in England, controlled a large source of income. Wolsey built 1,000 rooms, but it was confiscated by Henry VIII and became a royal palace.

2. Wollaton Hall, Nottinghamshire. Built around 1580 it contains a spectacular central hall rising above the surrounding buildings. It was designed by Robert Smythson who also designed Longleat House.

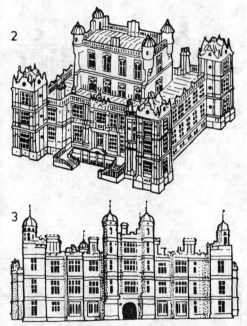

3. Burghley House, Stamford, Northamptonshire.
Built by Sir William Cecil, principal adviser to Queen
Elizabeth I, this is an excellent example of a 16th-
century courtyard house.

1. Charlton House, Kent. Built in 1607, the use of dark brick with light stone detail for window surrounds and corner and parapet features make a striking pattern of simple shapes.

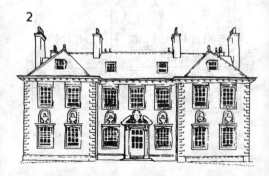

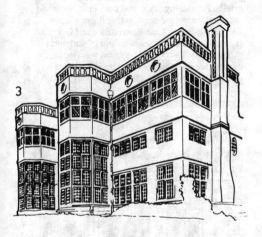

2. Honington Hall, Warwickshire. Built in 1685 of brick, with stone used for corners, cornices, and door and window frames. The facade has a strong sense of symmetry.

3. Astley Hall, Chorley, Lancashire. A unique Stuart period house built in 1655. Now covered by plaster, the very few parts of the building that are walls were initially brickwork. The enormous pair of ground-floor windows make the interior very dazzling and bright.

From this time onwards architects (rather than their patrons) were the arbiters of architectural forms and details. Personality, style, and both innovation and imitation were the determining influences upon architectural style. Late Renaissance and Georgian architects used buildings as a form of sculptural expression of their ideas. Function was frequently overshadowed by form, where buildings were created for their aesthetic value rather than solely for utility.

Seaton Delaval, Northumberland. Sir John Vanbrugh's Baroque building of 1718 was designed with little concession to domesticity. The use of large blocks of heavily textured masonry (rustication) creates a dramatic effect.

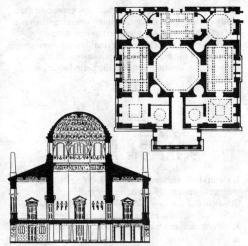

Chiswick House, Hounslow, London. In 1725, Lord Burlington and William Kent devised a charming villa based upon a house designed by Palladio at Vicenza, Italy. Although used in the 18th century as a residence, it was never intended to be one. Here, amid quiet parkland, friends and guests came to admire imported Italian sculptures and paintings and listen to refined musical recitals. The plan above reveals how the architect designed a building in which the size, shape and position of the rooms were the consequence of aesthetic ideas rather than practical needs.

While 19th-century industrial buildings expressed the purity of functional design, architects building domestic and religious buildings attempted to imitate and combine every conceivable previous architectural style. Classical, Norman, Gothic, Renaissance – all had revivals. But shorter more specific period styles were also flaunted.

1. Cronkhill, Shropshire, 1802. John Nash, a Regency architect, was capable of designing buildings in both Classical and Gothic styles. This house, although built in 1802, is an Italian villa incorporating large Mediterranean eaves and basic geometric forms.

2. Harlaxton Manor, Lincolnshire, 1830s. Designed by Anthony Salvin, in an Elizabethan style. The house is seen beyond the forecourt gates and screen.

3. Castell Coch, near Cardiff, South Glamorgan, 1872. The invention of the architect William Burges, who recreated a medieval world for Lord Bute. It features 13th-century style European turrets, high circular towers with enormous footings, a drawbridge and battlements with arrow slits for windows.

4. Elvetham Hall, Hampshire, 1859. Built by S.S. Teulon for Lord Calthorpe it displayed an idiosyncratic use of medieval architectural styles. Coloured bands of brick work, stained glass, cluttered turrets and chimneys make this a fairyland.

Council Developments: Cwmbran New Town, Gwent, 1946. The Housing Act of 1919 provided for new state-funded housing, which resulted in the building of vast expanses of council housing in the 1920s and 30s. After the Second World War governments further encouraged municipal housing programmes.

Speculative Developments: Crawley New Town, West Sussex, 1969. Large building contractors purchased land, which, when divided into very small plots, covered with inexpensive two-storey houses, provided individual ownership for the new white-collar workers of the 1960s and 70s.

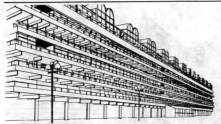

Urban Revitalization: The Barbican, London, 1982.
With planning starting in 1957, and its completion in
1982, the Barbican development is a typical example of
urban revitalization. Inner-city urban decay, bombing of
cities during the Second World War, and later
accelerating property values have meant opportunities
for municipal authorities and property developers to
demolish the centres of the cities and rebuild new urban
residential complexes.

**New Technologies, Satellite Cities: Runcorn New
Town, Cheshire, 1970s.** Many architects have applied
the new technologies of metal cladding and industrial
design to residential housing. The new dormitory towns
of Runcorn, Milton Keynes, Harlow and Cumbernauld
are attempts to solve existing inner-city congestion by
situating urban infrastructure in rural settings.

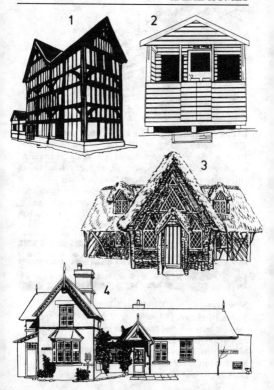

1. Hunting Lodge, Epping Forest, Essex. The weekend retreat for Elizabeth I, from which she and her party could hunt in the vast expanse of Epping Forest.

2. Seaside Changing Hut, Walton-on-the-Naze, Essex. The 1920s saw the growth of small timber one-roomed dwellings where weekenders could rest after a day spent sunbathing, swimming and playing on the beach.

3. Swiss Chalet, Shrivenham, Berkshire, 1850. A replica of the chalet in which Lord Barrington stayed during his honeymoon in Switzerland.

4. Station House, Onibury, Shropshire, 1865. Once a railway station, now a country home; the ticket office is a living room, the waiting room now the kitchen.

5. Bridgeman's Cottage, Stroud, Gloucestershire, 1827. This cottage shows the transformation of plain local styles to fashionable Regency modes.

The Royal Pavilion, Brighton, Sussex, 1817.
Designed by John Nash this is a magnificent palace
which features Indian-style domes and minarets on the
outside, and Chinese-style decorations on the inside.

The Casino at Marino House, Dublin, 1769. A
miniature dwelling; the urns on the roof are chimneys.

The Triangular Lodge, Rushton, Northamptonshire, 1594. Sir Thomas Tresham, a noted Roman Catholic recusant, built a house of stone, whose plan, roofs, windows and decorations reflect the sacred Holy Trinity. It has three sides, each with three windows and three gables.

2. Religious buildings

Pre-Roman religious buildings have survived as gaunt exposed structures in remote locations. Probably, when constructed, they were centres of thriving agricultural communities.

As no records of the events of the 3,000 years of pre-Roman construction survived, many of the functions of the buildings have to be guessed at. Mounds were constructed as burial chambers; groups of stones set in circles or lines, it is assumed, were astronomic calenders and temples to the gods of seasonal forces; dolmens or cromlechs – groups of stones supporting a flat stone – were probably exposed structures of a burial mound.

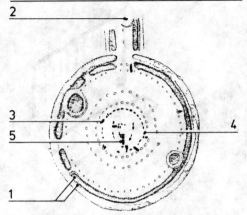

Stonehenge, Wiltshire. Begun about 4,500 years ago, Stonehenge is depicted opposite as it would have appeared in about 1550 BC. This Bronze Age temple was used by the inhabitants of south-west England for around 1,000 years.

The outer earthworks (**1**) consisting of a ditch and bank were built in approximately 2500 BC. The Heel Stone (**2**) indicates the position of the rising sun on the longest day of the year, and was positioned at the time of building the ditch and bank. The blue-stone inner ring (**3**) was constructed around 2100 BC; sarsen stones replaced some of the blue-stones in about 2000 BC. A blue-stone circle (**4**) was added to the centre, and an altar stone (**5**) set up in approximately 1550 BC.

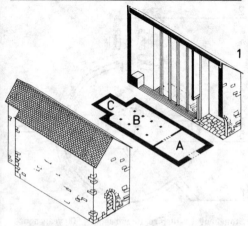

1. Roman Mithraic Temple. These small buildings
(dedicated to the worship of the Persian god Mithras)
were the original influence on early Christian churches
in Britain.

The entrance led to a small initiation hall (the narthex)
(**A**), then to a nave (similar to those found in today's
parish churches) (**B**), and finally to the altars in the
west end (the sanctuary) (**C**).

2. Celtic Monastery, Skellig Michael, Co. Kerry.
Early Christian missionaries built small stone cells –
like this 6th- or 7th-century construction – for
themselves and converts. Most were destroyed by
Nordic raiders.

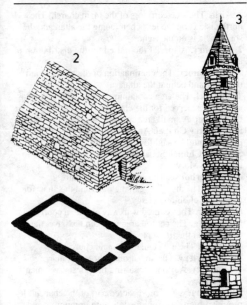

3. Priest's Round Tower, Brechin, Tayside. Built mostly in Ireland in the 9th and 10th centuries, this is one of the two remaining Scottish towers. As defence against the Nordic raiders they may have saved the occupants, but they did little to protect the monastic buildings which the invaders usually sacked and burnt.

1. Aisle. The side corridors of the main church. The north aisle is on the left when facing the altar, and the south aisle is on the right.

2. Almonry. A special room used for the distribution of alms.

3. Ambulatory. The continuation of the aisle around the choir and behind the altar.

4. Chancel. The area containing the choir and the altar, originally reserved for the clergy.

5a. Chapel. A small area set aside for private worship.

5b. Chantry Chapel. An endowed chapel in which prayers could be said for the soul of the benefactor.

5c. Lady Chapel. Set at the east end and dedicated to the Virgin Mary.

6. Chapterhouse. The administrative centre.

7. Choir. The area between the nave and the altar, for use by the choir and clergy.

8. Cloister. The covered walkway around a courtyard.

9. Crossing. The central area between the nave, the chancel and the transept.

10. Crypt. The area under the main church.

11. Presbytery. The area around the main altar.

12. Sacristy. A room for storing the priests' vestments and sacred vessels.

13. Sanctuary. The most sacred part of the chancel. It provided fugitives from the law with immunity from arrest.

14. Nave. The main area of the church used by the congregation. It usually has aisles on either side.

15. Slype. A passageway from cloister to transept or chapterhouse.

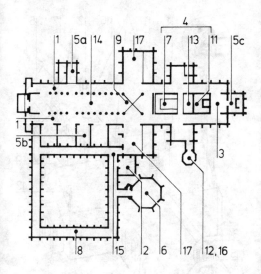

16. Vestry. Another term for the sacristy, where vestments and sacred vessels are kept.
17. Transept. The two areas on either side of the crossing, which form part of the cross-shaped plan of the church.

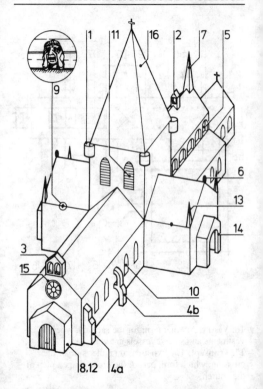

1. Bartizan. A small turret projecting from a wall, parapet or tower.

2. Bellcote. A bell tower on a roof.

3. Bell Gable. A bell tower mounted on the end wall.

4a. Buttress. A masonry support against a wall.

4b. Flying Buttress. A support which is arched so that the brace is away from the wall.

5. Clerestory. A row of windows in the upper part of a wall, above the roof of an aisle.

6. Finial. An ornament on top of buildings.

7. Fleche. A small wooden spire.

8. Galilee. An enclosed porch at the west end of the church.

9. Gargoyle. A spout carrying water from the roof, usually decorated with a grotesque figure or head.

10. Lancet. A tall and narrow pointed window.

11. Louvre. A window opening, in church towers, covered with overlapping boards.

12. Narthex. A porch at the west end of a church.

13. Pinnacle. A small stone spire on top of buttresses, parapets or roofs.

14. Porch. An entrance that is covered.

15. Rose Window. A circular window.

16. Spire. A tall, pointed structure, most commonly found on a tower.

1. Altar. The table at the east end of the church from which acts of worship are conducted. It is divided from the choir by rails.

2. Brasses. Engraved brass plates attached to tombs. They usually depict the deceased.

3. Canopy. A small protective hood usually placed over a pulpit or tomb.

4. Choir Screen. The partition, usually of wood, between the choir stalls and the nave of the church.

5. Easter Sepulchre. A recess in the north chancel to hold the effigy of the risen Christ used during Easter celebrations.

6. Credence. A small table or shelf on which is placed the bread and wine used for communion service.

7. Font. A large raised fixed basin containing holy water used for baptisms.

8. Funeral. Usually wooden painted shields called "hatchments" bearing the arms of deceased local gentry.

9. Lectern. A desk or stand designed to hold a bible or large service book.

10. Misericord. A ledge, often decorated and carved, projecting from the underside of a hinged seat, built to support a standing person.

11. Pew. Wooden seating for the congregation.

12. Piscina. A stone basin with a drain placed near the altar and used for washing the sacred vessels.

13. Pulpit. An elevated platform, often approached by a flight of steps, from which the congregation is addressed.

14. Reredos. A decorated screen behind the altar.

15. Rood. A cross or crucifix placed in the east part of the nave and in front of the choir stalls.

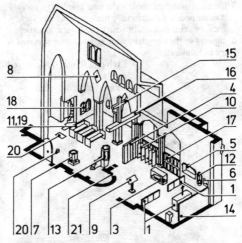

16. Roodscreen. The support to the rood, often in elaborately carved wood or stone.

17. Screen. A parclose screen is one around an altar or shrine.

18. Sedilia. Seats for the clergy, often recessed into the wall.

19. Stall. Another name for a pew.

20. Stoup. Basin of holy water near the church entrance.

21. Squirt. A small slit in the wall or pier to enable members of the congregation (usually lepers in a separate room) to have sight of the altar.

Within a churchyard there were small buildings serving particular needs. Occasionally there were charnel houses, or skull houses, in which the bones of earlier occupants of the cemetery were stored – one survives at Bury St Edmunds.

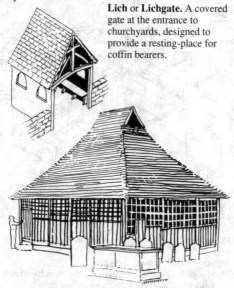

Lich or **Lichgate.** A covered gate at the entrance to churchyards, designed to provide a resting-place for coffin bearers.

Bell House, East Bergholt, Suffolk. A single-storey belfry built to house five of England's heaviest bells.

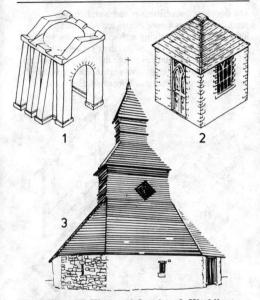

Watch Boxes: 1. Wanstead, London; 2. Warblington, Hertfordshire. Eighteenth-century sentinel boxes for protecting the cemetery from body-snatchers.
3. Bell Tower, Pembridge, Herefordshire. Built to house heavy bells when it was expected that the construction of a church tower would not be possible on the site of the current church.

The development of British church architecture
produced changes whose names are now used for
identifying and classifying architectural styles. Pages 8
to 10 contain a list of styles and their periods.
Of Anglo-Saxon churches before the Norman conquest
only the stone buildings survive, with the exception of
parts of the wooden nave of Greensted, Essex.

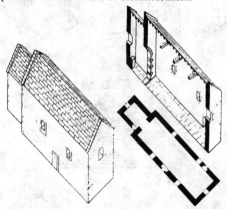

Escomb, Bishop Auckland, Durham. The earliest
Christian churches had a similar plan to small Roman
temples. Escomb is a rare surviving example from the
early 8th century.
Other Saxon churches survive at Bradford-on-Avon,
Wiltshire; Dover, Kent; Barton-on-Humber,
Lincolnshire; and Bradwell-on-Sea, Essex.

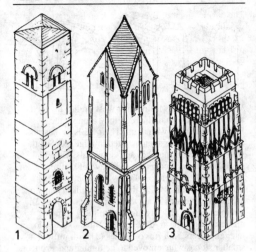

Anglo-Saxon Towers

The three church towers above (not drawn to common scale) show the development from the simple box structure of Monkwearmouth to the elaborate decorative stonework of Earls Barton.

1. Monkwearmouth, Sunderland, Tyne and Wear.
Built about the year 900.

2. Sompting, Sussex. Built also about the year 900.

3. Earls Barton, Northamptonshire. Built about 100 years later, in approximately 1000.

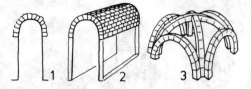

When the Normans from north-west France invaded and conquered Britain in 1066 they brought the Romanesque style with them. Their skills as masons and engineers were demonstrated in large, powerful, well-constructed churches and cathedrals. They had perfected the roof-covering technique of vaulting developed 1,000 years earlier by the Romans.
This initially consisted of the use of semicircular stone arches (**1**) extended along the length of covering (**2**); but intersecting aisles required extremely complex masonry skills to carve stones that fitted exactly, so later engineers built ribs of arches (**3**) with infilled smaller stones which proved to be lighter and stronger.

Features:

1. Walls. Thick, smooth-faced, rectangular-dressed large stones with an infilling of small stones, and broad but shallow buttresses.

2. Windows. Narrow and semicircular (**a**), usually with the inside wall widely splayed (**b**).

3. Doors. Surrounded by semicircular arches, often colourfully decorated with a zigzag and dog-tooth pattern.

4. Capitals. Either square with cushion-type decoration, or circular.

5. Columns. Massive circular structures, sometimes covered with ascending spirals or diamonds.

6. Bases. Circular, set on square footings.

7. Mouldings. Appeared in the following geometric styles: **a.** chevron or zigzag; **b.** billet.

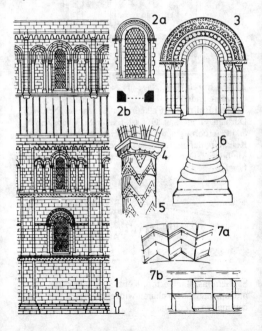

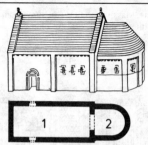

Basic Church Plan. Nave (**1**), sanctuary – either round or square ended (**2**).

Typical Buildings: Cathedrals at Chichester, Norwich, Durham, Gloucester, Oxford, Exeter, St Albans, Ely and Peterborough; and the churches at Barfreston, Kent; circular church, Cambridge; Iffley at Oxford; Melbourne, Derbyshire; and the chapel in the Tower of London.

St Nicholas, Barfreston, Kent. Simple box-like monumental parish church with examples of fine stone carving.

Iffley Church, Oxford, Oxfordshire. The west front was built in 1170.

Melbourne Church, Derbyshire. Begun in 1100 and finished 40 years later. It contains a small but striking interior with massive columns and simple surface decoration.

The records in the Domesday Book (1086) show that there were almost as many churches in England then as were recorded nearly 700 years later in a 1750's survey.

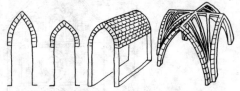

Builders encountering difficulties with the problems of creating intersecting spaces with aisles of two different widths solved the problem either by constructing pointed arches (as the height of pointed arches is not determined by their width), or by raising the level of the springers (the bottom stones) on the narrower semicircular arch.

Churches after the 12th century contained lighter, thinner structures with aisles and naves of varying width. To support the increased height and thinness of many walls, the flying buttress was introduced, which transferred the downward thrusts out to supports and away from the main inner wall, allowing construction with larger windows.

Features:

1. Walls. More graceful than Norman. Thinner with lighter structures because of increased window space. The first flying buttresses.

2. Windows. Tall, set in groups with a thin, solid section above called "plate tracery". The beginning of the use of the pointed arch.

3. Doors. Because of pointed arches, the width of doors no longer needed to relate to the height of the arch, giving the entrances a more graceful appearance.

4. Capitals. Foliage and natural forms in deep relief.

5. Columns. Circular or octagonal, with accompanying shafts.

6. Bases. Simply set, on square or round footings.

7. Mouldings: a. lively naturalistic elements; **b.** regular repeat patterns of foliage.

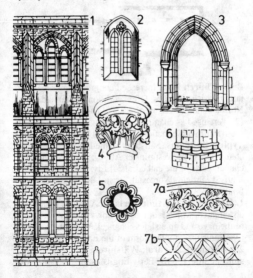

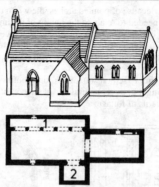

Basic Church Plan. Increased congregations meant
larger parish churches. Often additions were made to a
Norman church. The north aisle (**1**) and south chapel
(**2**) were used as chantries, and such additions were
often built with donations from local wealthy families.
Typical Buildings: Salisbury Cathedral; the
chapterhouse of Westminster Abbey; Lambeth Palace
chapel; parts of the cathedrals of Ely, Lincoln, York,
Wells, Lichfield, Worcester, Bristol, Rochester and
Southwick.

1. Haltwhistle, Northumberland. A simple plan of an
aisled nave, which required windows in the upper part
of the nave and an aisleless chancel. Without a tower it
represents the simplest form of the Early English style.

2. Salisbury Cathedral, Wiltshire. Built in 1220–58
almost entirely in the Early English style. It displays all

the main features of the period: pointed arches, a high roof, lancet windows and the use of flying buttresses.

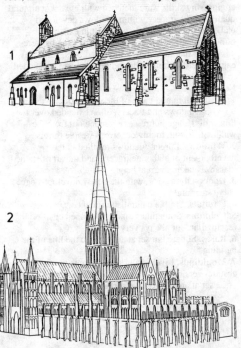

The 14th-century builders felt free to add decoration to all the surfaces of their buildings. Advanced engineering skills were matched with greater sculptural qualities. The tracery within windows developed elaborate curves and delicacy. Within existing buildings, delicately carved shrines and tombs were conceived like miniature buildings. Fonts, gargoyles, eagle lecterns, choir stalls and pulpits were also added to enrich the interior.

Features:

1. Walls. More and more of the wall surface was taken up with windows and tracery, often extended over the thin walls. Stage buttresses extended out from the walls, often with highly decorated steeple turrets.

2. Windows. Larger windows resulted in the development of elaborate tracery, and the art of stained glass was taken to great heights.

3. Doors. Often wide, with the newly developed ogee curve surround.

4. Capitals. Simple naturalistic foliage.

5. Columns. Sometimes diamond-shaped or rectangular, but always very fluted.

6. Bases. Square but set at an angle to the line of the building.

7. Mouldings. Lively naturalistic forms: **a.** mixed with abstract versions of balls and flowers; **b.** patterns were often set at an angle to the surface.

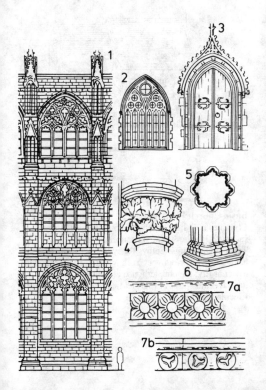

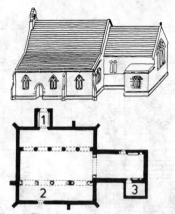

Basic Church Plan. Introduction of a north porch (**1**). Churches now have north and south aisles (**2**), and a sacristy (**3**) is built onto a chancel.

Typical Buildings: Selby Abbey; Exeter Cathedral; the nave and west window at York Minster; the octagonal tower at Ely; the chapterhouse at Southwell Minster; the nave and spires at Lichfield; and the choir stalls at Lincoln Cathedral.

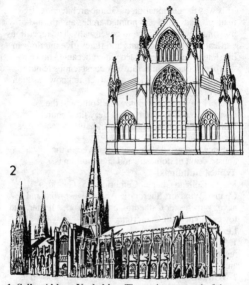

1. Selby Abbey, Yorkshire. The entire east end of the choir is taken up with a single window. Displaying great confidence in building skills, the tracery forms no main structural purpose as the roof is clearly supported by the aisles and buttresses.

2. Lichfield Cathedral, Staffordshire. Graceful central and western spires in decorated style form the only triple group of spires in England.

This was the culmination of Gothic architecture. It featured flatter and less pointed arches and the use of maximum window space to cover walls. The repetitious vertical mouldings, colours and flutes give interiors an illusion of heightened space which became known as "perpendicular architecture". A conspicuous feature was the elaborate interior roof structure known as "fan tracery".

After Henry VIII's dispute with Rome and the destruction of the monasteries, very little church building or work on cathedrals and abbeys took place for 100 years.

The newly created style was employed in the construction of domestic and civic buildings.

Typical Buildings:

King's College Chapel, Cambridge; St George's Chapel, Windsor; Sherborne Abbey; west front and nave, Winchester Cathedral; choir of York Minster; and tower and nave of Canterbury.

Features:

1. **Walls.** Probably decorated with panelling that resembles window tracery, repeated vertical decoration and wide-reaching buttresses.

2. **Windows.** The curved and straight arch, known as the four-centred arch, became the main feature on doors and windows, and often occupied all the wall.

3. **Doors.** The tops of the doors appeared in the new window style, often with a protruding moulding set across the opening.

4. **Capitals.** Polygonal in plan.

5. **Columns.** Often thin groups of shafts set in diamond formations at frequent intervals along side walls.

6. Bases. Polygonal in plan.

7. Mouldings. These became less obtrusive, shallow but with a simple directness of style. They featured:

a. natural foliage turned into geometric patterns; or,

b. were modified like the Tudor Rose, a symbol of the power of the crown.

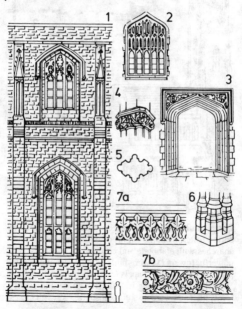

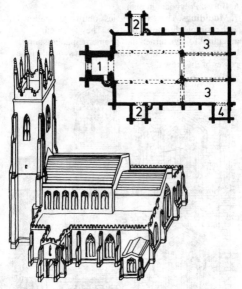

Basic Church Plan. Increased wealth during the Tudor period (often from the export of wool) endowed small churches with elaborate and complex elements. New powerful towers (**1**) were built, north and south porches (**2**), north and south chapels (**3**), and chantry chapels (**4**). With donations coming in from rich guilds and Tudor lords, interiors were also embellished.

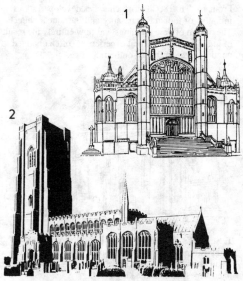

1. St George's Chapel, Windsor, Berkshire. Begun in 1475, within the castle walls of Windsor, it was intended as a memorial to the victories of Edward IV but was not completed till 1528.

2. Lavenham, Suffolk. An enormously rich parish church built in the late 15th century. Bristling with adornments from the wool trade merchants it stands on a hill outside the village.

From 1600 to 1800 British churches developed styles imitative of Italian Renaissance and Baroque architects. The design of new buildings was now entirely the result of individual and cultural experience – often obtained on tours of central and southern Europe.

1

1. St Paul's, Covent Garden, London. A theatre set and costume designer, Inigo Jones, in 1630 made the small church in Covent Garden known as "the most handsomest barn in the kingdom".

2. St Paul's Cathedral, London. Christopher Wren's greatest and largest religious building. Its dome, completed in 1710, dominated the London skyline for 200 years. After the Great Fire of London in 1666, in which the old St Paul's was badly damaged, a tax on coal imported to London raised money for the construction of a monument befitting the phoenix of the burnt Gothic ashes.

3. St Paul's Dome, London.

Wren devised three domes for the cathedral. The inner (**A**) is of brick and covers the church crossing. The interior dome (**B**) is conical brick, with iron chains used to retain the overall structure. The outer dome (**C**) is a timber and lead structure.

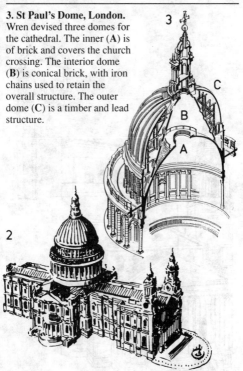

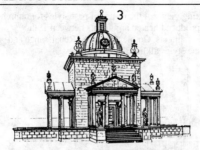

1. St Lawrence, West Wycombe, Buckinghamshire.
The local landowner, Sir Francis Dashwood, had this
Christian church with pagan influences built in 1763. It
contains a nave modelled on the Temple of the Sun at
Palmyra, Italy, and a spire surmounted by a golden ball
in which it was alleged that members of the Hell Fire
Club (to which Dashwood belonged) would meet.

2. St George's, Bloomsbury, London. Nicholas
Hawksmoor designed this imposing monumental town
church, built between the years 1720 and 1730, after
having worked with two of Britain's most famous
Baroque architects, Sir Christopher Wren and Sir John
Vanbrugh.

3. The Temple, Castle Howard, Yorkshire. This is the
Temple of the Four Winds by Sir John Vanbrugh, built
in 1700. It is not a church, but is included here because,
in the late 17th century, powerful landowners like the
3rd Earl of Carlisle could commission architects to
design religious buildings which have no Christian
connotations.

Conflicting views of the re-use of past styles for church design produced heated arguments between 19th-century architects. Gothic, Classical, Renaissance and Byzantine styles all had their exponents.

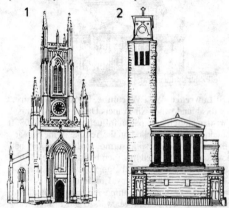

1. St Peter's, Brighton, East Sussex. Built in 1824 to the design of Sir Charles Barry. A fine example of the early Victorian Gothic revival style.

2. Caledonia Road Free Church, Glasgow, Strathclyde. A Greek temple raised above street level, designed by Alexander "Greek" Thomson in 1856 as a "modern" building with Classical detailing.

3. Hoarwithy, Herefordshire. An Italianate tower and nave built in the 1880s. It is to be found perched on the top of a hill near Ross-on-Wye.

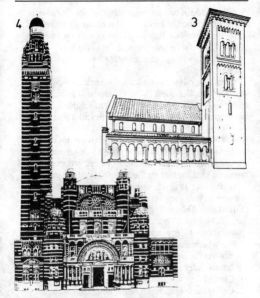

4. Westminster Cathedral, London. After 300 years of Protestant domination the Roman Catholics were, in 1829, allowed to practise their own religion and build their own churches.

This Byzantine-style cathedral (built between 1895 and 1903) was consecrated in 1910 and is the headquarters of the Roman Catholic Church in Britain.

Until the 1530s and the dissolution of the monasteries in Britain, much of medieval church architecture was directed to the building of groups of religious buildings, which served religious purposes but also had accommodation and amenities for a community of monks and nuns.

The earliest monastic settlements, such as those before the Norman Conquest (1066), were built in Ireland, the west coast of Scotland, and northern England. These were groups of individual cells with small places of worship.

From Norman times up to 1539 the two main religious orders were the Benedictines and the Cistercians. In both establishments the buildings were grouped around an open area located on the south side of the main church nave. This was circled by an open arcade or cloister giving the occupants an area of privacy.

Fountains Abbey, Yorkshire. Now a ruin but once a grand complex of buildings. Completed in 1160 it had a population of Cistercian monks who controlled a vast estate which included sheep farms and iron and lead mines. At the peak of their power they were the richest religious order in England.

1. Church.

2. Cellarium. The storehouse containing crops harvested by the monks and goods paid to the abbey by tenants of abbey lands.

3. Kitchens. Where food for all occupants was prepared.

4. Refectory. The large private dining room for the monks.

5. Hospice. The guest house for travellers, a hospital and an alms house for the sick and destitute.
6. Abbot's House. The house of the presiding authority of the monastery.
7. Monks' Infirmary. Private hospital.
8. Lay Brothers' Infirmary. Infirmary for new monks.
9. Monks' Dormitory. Private living quarters.
10. Cloister.
In addition there were brewhouses, a mill, fishponds and farm buildings.

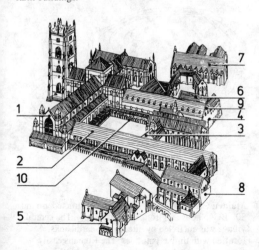

3. Military and military-style buildings

Castles and defence systems become obsolete when
advances in military technology render them irrelevant,
or the political reasons for their construction evaporate.
Throughout the British Isles, their remains bear witness
to historical change.

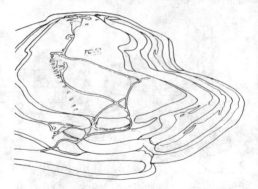

Maiden Castle, Dorset. A hill fort constructed around
300 BC to house an Iron Age community. The central
village was encircled by ditches and earthbanks,
fortified with timber palisades. The Romans easily
overran these and sacked the fortress in AD 43.

Broch, Jarlshof, Shetland. Unique to Scotland, these towers and enclosures were built by Celtic farmers as protection against invaders and other raiders. The high tower would have served as a lookout and the thick walls (as the section of the base shows) were impregnable against attack by sling shot, arrows or spears.

Roman military buildings were located strategically over the length of Roman Britain, and also appeared in Scotland. The main defence structure was Hadrian's Wall, extending from Carlisle to Newcastle, built to protect the northern borders of the conquered island. Most Roman structures have been vandalized over the last 1,500 years, as their dressed stone could be used for later buildings.

1

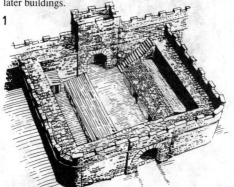

1. A "Mile Castle", Cumbria. A small fortified gateway in Hadrian's Wall through which local people passed daily. Each mile castle would house 8 to 32 Roman soldiers.

2. Benwell, Northumberland. A garrison fort set astride Hadrian's Wall. From here legions of soldiers could be quickly dispatched to any part of the wall under threat of attack.

2

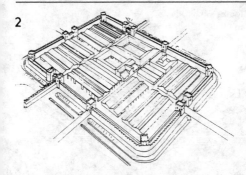

3. Garrison Gate, South Shields, Tyne and Wear.
Built originally in AD 161, reconstruction shows the
power of Roman defences.
Before the invention of artillery, these thick, high stone
walls offered impregnable positions for occupying
forces. This fort had 22 granaries and was used as the
supply base for soldiers serving further north in
Scotland.

3

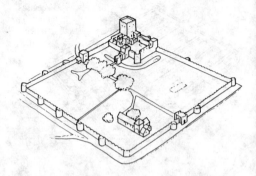

Porchester Castle, Hampshire. A Roman fort on the
south coast of England built as a defence against
invasion by Saxon pirates.

The Romans built protruding towers along the
perimeter wall to give them clear views from which to
fire arrows or stones from a ballista. It would have been
garrisoned by approximately 1,000 legionaries.

There are other forts at Burgh in Suffolk; Bradwell-
juxta-Mare (Bradwell-on-Sea) in Essex; Reculver,
Richborough and Lymphe in Kent; and at Pevensey in
Sussex. The upkeep of forts was costly and they were
vulnerable to raids by mobile bands of Saxon invaders.
Porchester was occupied, subsequent to the Romans
leaving Britain, by later invaders such as the Saxons
and the Normans. The aerial view shows the Norman
keep, inner bailey and the Augustinian priory church,

founded in 1133. The present 12th-century tower uses the high ground corner of the Roman encampment. The old Roman wall was used as an outer bailey defence system. The castle was further reinforced in the 14th century.

Burgh Castle, Suffolk. A rare, surviving example of the walls of a Roman coastal fort. It is now, however, 3 miles inland. Burgh Castle was built during the 3rd century as a defence against Saxon attacks. The three surviving walls are constructed from flint, banded with narrow layers of brick. When first constructed, the walls would have been 25 feet high and between 12 and 15 feet thick.

1. Watchtower. Usually the tallest turret on a keep or wall.

2. Keep. The strongest building in the castle.

3. Flanking Tower. Protruding from the wall to enable archers to provide cover along the castle walls.

4. Inner Bailey. The area closest to the keep, usually separated from the outer bailey by an inner ring of defensive walls.

5. Angle Tower. Positioned on corners to enable the archers to cover two sides of a castle.

6. Gatehouse. Defences over a gate.

7. Portcullis. Heavy gate which could be lowered when castle was under attack.

8. Causeway. The approach to the entrance.

9. Drawbridge. The entrance platform over a ditch or moat which could be raised if under attack.

10. Ramparts. The defence walls or castle battlements.

11. Palisade. Wooden defence walls.

12. Outer Bailey. The area outside the inner defences, protected by outer ramparts.

13. Scarp. Sloping land at the foot of the battlement walls.

14. Moat. Usually a man-made ditch with water that surrounds a castle.

15. Postern Gate (Sally Port). A small entrance to or exit from the castle away from the main gate.

16. Arrow Slits. Openings in the wall from which archers could fire at attackers.

17. Outer Curtain Wall. The outermost wall, usually linking turrets (bastions).

18. Bastion. An individual turret or tower on a wall.

19. Garderobe. A medieval lavatory.

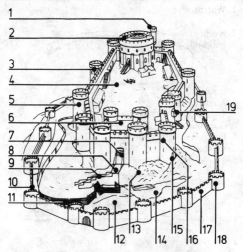

1
2
3
4
5
6
7
8
9
10
11
12 13 14 15 16 17 18
19

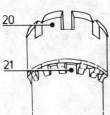

20
21

20. Crenellated Walls. The protruding walls provided archers with cover, whilst the gaps in between afforded them an opportunity to shoot at attackers.

21. Machicolation Holes. From which defenders could pour oil on, or fire arrows at, their attackers.

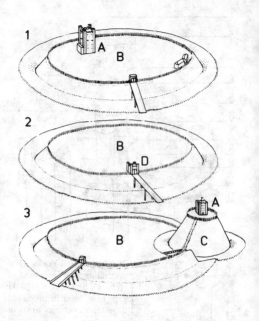

A. Keep
B. Bailey
C. Motte
D. Gatehouse/Keep

The defence of a homestead was usually via an encircling wooden fence, which was placed on the edge of a mound made from the earth dug from a ditch. A secret approach to the wooden wall would have been made more difficult by clearing away any trees or undergrowth and, if possible, flooding the ditch from a nearby stream or lake.

The area within the encirclement (called the bailey) would have had assorted domestic, agricultural and military buildings, as well as kennels, stables, armoury, workshop, brewhouse, bakehouse and chapel. In times of siege, neighbouring farmers would drive their livestock into the bailey and obtain protection from the lord in exchange for taking up arms in his defence. The defences developed first from simple encampments with a keep (the lord's residence). Later, powerful gate lodges and, finally, a small hill (a motte), on which the keep was built, were added.

1. Keep and Bailey Castles. Until the 11th century, the keep was usually a wooden structure but this proved to be a poor defence against besieging armies.

2. Gatehouse and Bailey Castle. Placing greater emphasis on the outer wall and gateway was a more likely way to ensure good defence.

3. Motte and Bailey Castle. By the 11th century, local barons preferred motte and bailey castles. The motte is a high mound of solid ground either fashioned from the surrounding irregular landscape or built as an earth mound. The keep surmounting the motte would have been of timber. Later, wooden structures were replaced with solid stone ones.

Castle keeps in the 12th century were the strong centres from which Normans dominated the surrounding, conquered Anglo-Saxons.

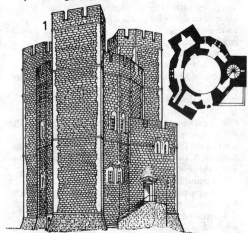

1. Orford Castle, Suffolk. Built in the 1160s, it still stands as an example of Henry II's originality in exploring keep design. It is circular (see section) with strong triangular elements formed by the three turrets.
2. Castle Hedingham, Essex. Built in 1140, it is a true Norman rectangular tower keep with corridors in the surrounding wall (see section) and elevated corner turrets for observation.

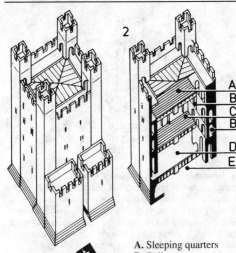

2

A. Sleeping quarters
B. Gallery
C. Hall
D. Garrison headquarters
E. Store rooms

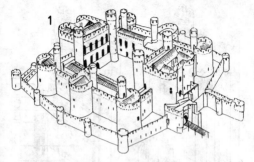

1. Beaumaris Castle, Anglesey. One of Edward I's range of castles intended to subdue the Welsh. It was begun in 1295 but construction stopped just under a century later, in the reign of Edward III. This drawing shows the intended height of the wall, turrets and other buildings. In the lower right-hand corner, you can see the fortified harbour, built to permit revictualling during a siege.

2. Castles Built or Strengthened by Edward I.
Edward I's castles in Wales were built or extensively renovated over a period of 25 years and are of four main types:

● Royal Marcher (border) castles at Chester, Shrewsbury, Montgomery and St Briavels.

■ Lordship castles (built and held by nobles, but constructed to the king's specification and partly financed by the crown) at Denbigh, Haward, Holt and Chirk.

△ Rebuilt captured Welsh castles, in particular those at Dolwyddelan, Criccieth and Bere.
▲ New castles at Builth, Aberystwyth, Flint, Rhuddlan, Ruthin, Hope, Conway, Harlech, Caernarvon and Beaumaris.
Beaumaris and Harlech (over page) were concentric castles, that is, built on a symmetrical plan with circular towers which were much harder to knock down than square ones. Both designs show that Edward I had been influenced by European, Crusader and Saracen fortifications encountered during the Second Crusade.

1

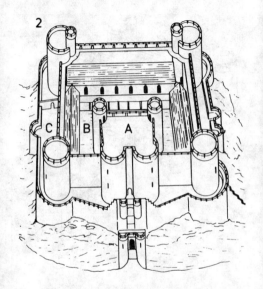

1. Caernarvon Castle, Gwynedd. This single-wall castle was begun in 1283; later castle designs (such as that for Harlech) featured an additional outer wall.
2. Harlech Castle, Gwynedd. Harlech was built in 1285. This view clearly shows the gatehouse keep (**A**), the inner courtyard (**B**), the outer courtyard (**C**) and the symmetrical plan.

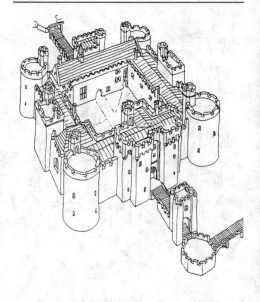

Bodiam Castle, Sussex. Built in 1388 to defend the surrounding stretch of south-east England under threat of French invasion during the Hundred Years War. It is a good example of a courtyard castle, surrounded by a moat. It was designed to provide a degree of residential comfort as well as defence.

1. Vicar's Peel, Corbridge, Northumberland. This 14th-century peel or pele is typical of the small fortified towers that were frequently built in the turbulent border area, between England and Scotland, fought over for the better part of 450 years. When raiders menaced, their approach could be signalled by the peel's lookout, and people and cattle could take refuge until armed help arrived.

2. Affleck Castle, Tayside. The section shows how security was provided, in the 15th century, by thick walls, small windows and rooms arranged vertically rather than side-by-side. The ground floor provided storage space and accommodated the guard, cattle and horses. On the first floor is the hall where eating and other daytime living activities took place. The chatelain (lord or laird) and his immediate family would have slept on the second floor. Each floor could be cut off from the one below it, if necessary.

1

Tower-Houses

Between 1560 and 1630, it became fashionable for the lesser gentry to build themselves tower-houses, using wealth newly acquired from the dissolution of the monasteries and the reapportioning of Roman Catholic Church lands, to enhance their social status.

The tower-house relied on the thickness of the walls, battlements and small grilled windows (which later generations enlarged). The rooms were still piled one on top of the other, each to be retreated into for last ditch defence.

1. Amisfield, Dumfries and Galloway. Built in 1650, this tower-house shows the "domestic" development that was incorporated into the upper floors. The windows, gable ends and turrets have all been decoratively embellished.

2. Claypotts, Tayside. Built in 1600, this displays an interesting feature in the bases of its walls – gun-loops.

1

Scotland had been influenced by French rather than English architectural styles well before the 17th century. The spindly towers and pepperpot turrets of the chateaux of Touranie were successfully transplanted onto the Scottish style.

1. Craigievar, Grampian. Built between 1610 and 1624, Craigievar remains substantially as it was when originally built, in the French style.

2. Glamis Castle, Tayside. Glamis was remodelled in the French style between 1650 and 1696.

Culzean, Strathclyde. Designed by Robert Adam and built between 1772 and 1792, Culzean is a Georgian mansion with Gothic embellishments.

Eastnor Castle, Hertfordshire. This is a castellated mansion of 1812 built in Norman and Gothic style, reflecting the architect's (Sir Robert Smirke) idea of a medieval castle and affirming the owner's equally ancient lineage.

Balmoral Castle, Grampian. Balmoral has been described as being a castle built from catalogues. The dream of "my dearest Albert", husband of Queen Victoria, who hankered after the Rhineland lodges of his youth. Rebuilt of white granite in the 1850s, it has become the summer home of the British royal family and their honoured guests.

Overtoun House, Strathclyde. Built for a private individual in 1858, the style can best be described as Scottish neo-baronial. A great many 16th- and 17th-century features are blended with those dictated by the ideals of mid-Victorian domestic comfort, albeit on a grand scale.

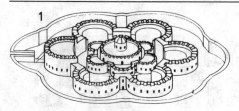

1. Deal Castle, Kent. One of the 20 forts designed specifically for artillery defence built in the 1540s by Henry VIII, who feared a French invasion. Deal Castle was built to accommodate 150 cannon. It held a small garrison, probably of no more than 24 soldiers and their captain, who lived in the central chambers.

The outer and lower rooms were used as kitchens and store rooms, and for ammunition. The various roof levels enabled the cannon, with limited elevation, to fire from different heights. In addition to the fixed and hand guns, there was a furnace for heating round-shot, which was particularly effective against wooden ships.

2. Fort George, Inverness-shire. Fort George was built between 1748 and 1760. It was built by William Adam (who died in 1748) and his sons. The designer was Colonel Skinner. Fort George should be seen in the context of the subjugation of the Highlands after the 1745 rebellion rather than the threat of French invasion.

3

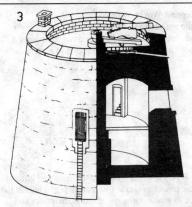

3. Martello Towers, South-East England. From 1793 up to the defeat of Napoleon at Waterloo in 1815, Britain was threatened with invasion by France. A defence cordon of round towers was built all over Britain and the Channel Islands. The examples in the south-east of England include towers at Seaford in Sussex and Aldeburgh in Suffolk.

The section shows the thick walls and the ground-floor living-quarters for troops. On the roof was a swivel-mounted cannon.

The Second World War

With the nation under siege from air attacks and possible coastal attacks, thousands of temporary structures utilizing new techniques and materials, were built.

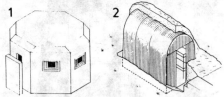

1. Pill Box. Concrete cabins cast *in situ* and built at strategic points to house small arms positions for the defence of roads, railways, airports, harbours and military or industrial installations.

2. Anderson Shelter. Sunk in pre-dug pits and covered with excavated earth, these personal family bunkers were erected everywhere against air attacks, mainly in suburban areas where gardens existed.

3. Thames Defences. Strange polypods of concrete erected in the Thames estuary as a defence against naval attack on London. Even today, they still stand as guardians of the river mouth.

4. Gun Emplacements. Vast concrete labyrinths of tunnelled defence buildings housing heavy artillery and mounted on cliffs and shores around Britain's coast.

5. Nissen Hut. Sectioned corrugated metal sheets which were bolted together to form temporary accommodation and storage.

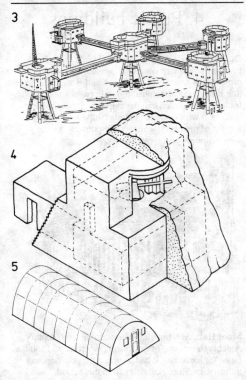

3

4

5

4. Public buildings

During the Middle Ages, increased trade brought prosperity. The rich beneficiaries naturally wished to protect their sources of wealth, so guilds were formed that restricted the membership or licenses sold to traders. The council hall developed at about the same time, also with restricted membership and elected or appointed members, who were responsible for the administration of the community.

Moot Hall, Aldeburgh, Suffolk. In the 16th century, Aldeburgh was one of the most prosperous ports on the East-Anglian coast. It had a successful ship-building industry. Its Moot Hall dates from this period.

Guildhall, Lavenham, Suffolk. England enjoyed great prosperity derived from the export of wool. The local Guild of Corpus Christi built the hall in 1529 alongside the Old Wool Hall, Tudor shops, and the house of the guild's founder, the 15th Lord de Vere.

Titchfield Market Hall. Now renovated and rebuilt at the Weald and Downland Open Air Museum, Chichester, West Sussex. Built soon after 1600, it is a timber-framed hall raised on wooden columns.

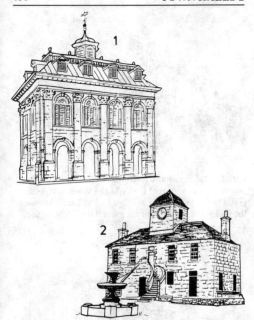

1. Town Hall, Abingdon, Oxfordshire. Rural prosperity, based on agricultural produce, developed into refinement and elegance. The town hall at Abingdon, built in 1682, has the character of a building designed by a sophisticated cosmopolitan architect.

2. Town Hall, Kintore, Grampian. Facing an open square, the first-floor entrance could be used for the delivery of proclamations or speeches by visiting dignitaries. Built in 1737, the use of such central clock towers later developed into vast spire-like structures.

3. Town Hall, Leeds, Yorkshire. Industrial prosperity, like agricultural wealth, can be used for civic pride. Leeds Town Hall, opened in the 1850s by Queen Victoria, was acclaimed as a monument to northern industrial power.

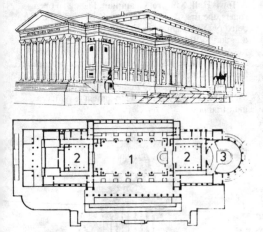

St George's Hall, Liverpool. The architect was commissioned to incorporate in one building a vast public hall (**1**) (over 151 feet long), for civic gatherings, two Assize Courts (**2**) and a concert hall (**3**). The building, completed in 1856, is a giant columned stone structure.

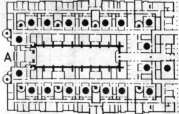

The Law Courts, London. The central offices of the
Supreme Court of Judicature for England and Wales
was opened in 1882. The irregular ornamental facade on
the Strand hides a vast complex of courts for
bankruptcy, admiralty, divorce, probate, Queen's Bench,
chancery and courts of appeal. The main entrance is the
large arch (**A**). The plan above has the courts marked
with black dots.

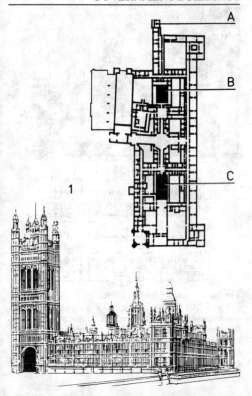

A

B

C

1

1. Houses of Parliament, London. Replacing the old Royal Palace of Westminster, which burnt down in 1834, the present buildings were assembled in the 1840s and 50s by the architects Sir Charles Barry and A.W.N. Pugin. The clock tower (**A**), just visible at the back of this drawing, became an international symbol for time, as it houses the bell affectionately known as Big Ben. The buildings are arranged around thirteen courtyards and at the centre of the complex are the two Houses of Parliament: the Commons (**B**) and the Lords (**C**).

2. 10 Downing Street, London. The official residence of the Prime Minister of Britain, with the most famous frontdoor in the land. This 18th-century house was formerly two houses, and its front is in fact the altered back of the house. An unpretentious face to a complex of rooms which serves as the government's nerve centre.

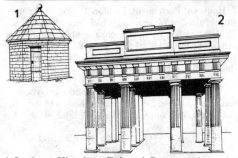

1. Lock-up, Kingsbury Episcopi, Somerset. An example of a village lock-up used to house malefactors prior to trial and exposure to the stocks or whipping post.

2. Chester Castle, Chester, Cheshire. The castle at Chester was built between 1788 and 1822 (the time of the French Revolution and the Napoleonic Wars) to house the county courts, the barracks and the prison. As the gateway (above) illustrates, Neo-Classicism prevailed in the design of Chester Castle. Civic power had to be seen to be in control.

3. Pentonville Prison, London. At the beginning of the 19th century, humanitarian concern began to influence prison design. Punishment in dark communal dungeons was superseded by the principle of social correction in airy buildings. The plan of Pentonville, which was built in 1840, shows the key idea of a central core with radial cell blocks, devised to provide maximum ventilation and light, individual cells and corridors for supervision.

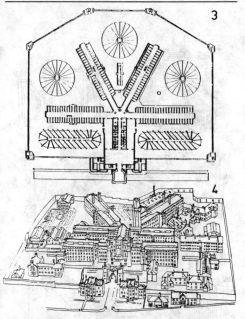

4. Holloway Prison, London. Built in 1849 to house 300 female prisoners, this aerial view shows the radial arrangement of the cell blocks, and the surrounding service buildings including the laundry, workshops, hospital, kitchens and administration.

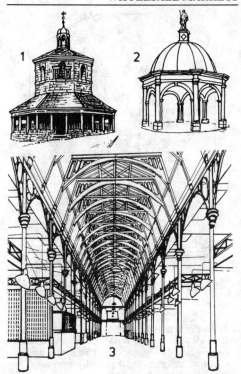

The right to trade was usually a highly protected privilege: the charters, granted by early monarchs, are still used to enable towns and cities to have either wholesale or retail markets. Taxes were often paid on imported goods and, before concern for public hygiene became a conditioning factor, the raising of monetary revenue was the prime motive for the municipal building of market halls.

1. Butter Market, Barnard Castle, Durham.

2. Butter Market, Bungay, Suffolk. These were two small gathering halls where dairy produce could be sold to the public.

3. Smithfield Meat Market, London. The vast growth in population during the 18th and 19th centuries meant that London developed a series of wholesale markets for specialized goods: Billingsgate for fish; Covent Garden for vegetables and fruit; and Smithfield for meat. These markets, because they required daily deliveries, proved a source of urban congestion and so have now, with the exception of Smithfield, been moved out of the centre of London.

All the 19th-century market buildings, throughout the British Isles, were examples of the power and simplicity of cast-iron constructions using light metal frames which could be glazed over to create great houses of commerce.

In addition to retail and wholesale markets, trading in
commodities or currencies produced many impressive
civic buildings.

Ulster Bank, Belfast. The power of money in the 19th
century, obtained from the wealth created by the
Industrial Revolution and the growth of the British
Empire, meant that banks could demonstrate their
newly created wealth in lavish displays of monumental
architecture. This Northern Irish bank was built in 1860
when confidence in commerce was on the increase.

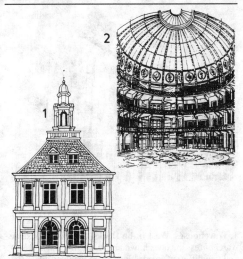

1. Customs House, King's Lynn, Norfolk. Import duties, tightly and easily controlled by coastal patrol, often led to prosperity for the local revenue office, as exemplified by this early (1681) quayside building.
2. Coal Exchange, London. Built in 1847 and demolished in the 1960s, it contained a central trading hall roofed by a delicate metal and glass dome. This and the Corn Exchange at Leeds were typical of halls for trading in commodities, where profits were made on confidence in the future value of the goods.

1. Warehouses, West India Docks, London. Dockside
warehouses (the one shown above was built in 1802–3)
had two different facades: one faced the quayside,
where goods from barges could be unloaded directly
into the building; on the other side, merchandise could
be lowered from any floor onto waiting horse-drawn
wagons for delivery. In these buildings, the goods could
be safely stored until import tax had been paid.
2. Warehouses, Stanley Dock, Liverpool. Although
a brick facade is shown, the buildings (1850–7) are
really constructed of cast-iron columns and frames.
Warehouse construction techniques later led to
the iron-framed skyscraper.

3. Warehouse and Shop, Glasgow, Strathclyde.
Although now a shopping area, this warehouse in
Jamaica Street, built in 1855, was once in a wholesale
commercial district. The street takes its name from the
West Indies' trade with Glasgow. It is a fine example of
the simplicity of cast-iron framed buildings.

As towns grew, so the need for individual shops selling specialized produce increased. The medieval shop was usually in the stores or workrooms which had ground-floor access.

1. Shops, Lavenham, Suffolk. A rare, surviving example of a medieval shop front, built in approximately 1500. The windows had shutters, half of which folded down to make counter surfaces, and half of which folded up to provide cover or shade.

2. Book Shop, Stamford, Lincolnshire. This example of an 18th-century shop reflects the refinement and taste, at that time, of the prosperous minority of provincial town dwellers.

3. Royal Arcade, London. Fashionable London, in the early part of the 19th century, required areas in which people could promenade and be seen by friends. Although built as late as 1879, the Royal Arcade still follows the elegant style of central London shopping arcades. This indoor idea of shopping has been extensively applied to the shopping centre of the 1970s.

The arrangement of the various elements of a college was first modelled on that of a monastic community: the main hall and buildings were grouped around a quadrangle in a manner resembling the arrangement of abbey and cloister. The major buildings included a hall, where staff and students dined together, the master's house, accommodation for staff, kitchens, accommodation for students and a library.

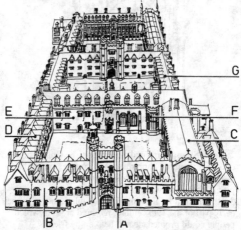

St John's College, Cambridge, Cambridgeshire. Founded in 1511. This is a fine example of the layout typically used for the Oxford and Cambridge colleges. The gateway (**A**) bears the arms of the founder, Lady

Margaret Beaufort (Henry VII's mother). The library (**B**), the chapel (**C**), chambers (**D**), kitchen (**E**) and hall (**F**) are all within the first quadrangle. The second quadrangle has the master's lodge (**G**) and further chambers. The third has additional accommodation.

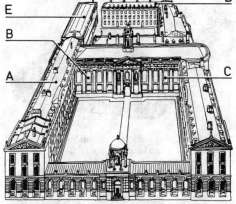

Queen's College, Oxford, Oxfordshire. Although built in the 1730s (200 years later than St John's College), the architect, Nicholas Hawksmoor, still retained the traditional arrangement of buildings.

The first quadrangle (viewed from the street) has the provost's lodge (**A**), hall (**B**) and chapel (**C**). The second quadrangle contains accommodation for staff and students (**D**), and a library (**E**) designed by Sir Christopher Wren.

Industrial-based prosperity, in cities such as Glasgow and the larger British towns, enabled local authorities to build schools and colleges which served particular needs.

1. Royal Holloway College, Egham, Surrey. Built in the 1880s, it is a vast educational establishment in the style of French chateaux.

2. Bonner Street Primary School, Hackney, London. The Education Act of 1870 resulted in towns in England constructing vast primary and secondary schools like this one, built in 1875. Initially, all were segregated with the boys and girls being educated and playing in separate areas.

3. Art School, Glasgow, Strathclyde. Famous when completed in 1896 for Charles Rennie Mackintosh's innovative Art Nouveau design. This building, with its high studio windows, has a very distinctive style, and is regarded as the most important "proto-modern" building in Britain.

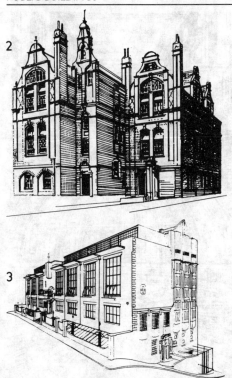

1▲

2▼

For a thousand years, the library system was in the hands of the monasteries. Almost all early libraries were wilfully destroyed during their dissolution in the 1530s. The surviving books were incorporated in royal, national or university libraries.

1. Trinity College Library, Cambridge, Cambridgeshire. One of the relatively few secular commissions executed by Sir Christopher Wren between 1676 and 1690. It is 150 feet long and built of a creamy-pink stone. The ground floor is open with a row of Tuscan columns in the centre. The library is on the upper floor.

2. The British Library Reading Room, Bloomsbury, London. A Neo-Classical circular domed building, the Reading Room was completed in 1857. The high curved and arched windows, in the dome, admit plenty of light. The layout of the floor is Victorian in design.

3. Radcliffe Camera, Oxford, Oxfordshire. Built in the 1740s, a rusticated base, supporting a Classical circular hall topped with a dome, makes this reading room resemble a Baroque church.

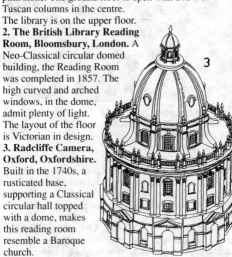

In the 19th century, public museums became a feature of most provincial cities, and two styles competed for their construction: the Classical and the Gothic. Within 25 years, from 1824 to 1850, four of Britain's major storehouses of artistic treasures were built.

1. **British Museum, London, 1824.**
2. **National Gallery, London, 1834.**
3. **Fitzwilliam Museum, Cambridge, Cambridgeshire, 1837.**
4. **National Gallery of Scotland, Edinburgh, 1850.**
Each has a Classical facade. The features of a Greek temple, with ascending stepped approaches, rows of columns with Doric or Corinthian capitals, friezes and pediments, were all employed to create temples of culture.
5. **University Museum, Oxford, Oxfordshire.** The spires, the pointed arches on windows and doors, the tracery and circular windows in the gabled ends are all

Gothic features. Inside the museum, the naturalistic foliage, once carved in stone in cathedrals, is here wrought in iron. While medieval builders strove to construct for the glory of God, here, in the centre of a university city, the architect constructs for the worship of knowledge.

6. Whitechapel Gallery, Whitechapel, London. By the end of the 19th century, architects and philanthropists were breaking with tradition. The Whitechapel Gallery was deliberately located to bring culture to the working classes and designed in defiance of both Gothic and Classical forms.

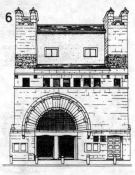

1. Royal Albert Hall, London. A vast concert hall which holds 8,000 people. Built in the 1860s as part of the Victorian ambition to develop Kensington into a cultural and educational campus.

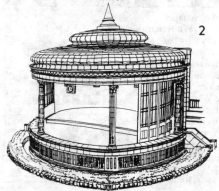

2. Bandstand, Eastbourne, East Sussex. The south-coast seaside resort has a bandstand around which 3,500 people on the Grand Parade can sit and listen to brass bands.

3. Royal Festival Hall, London. Built as a concert hall and part of the 1951 Festival of Britain (**A**), it was subsequently given a new face in the 1960s when tastes changed (**B**).

Roman Amphitheatre, Caerleon, Gwent.
A reconstruction of the 1st-century Roman stadium is
shown here. Owing to their extensive military presence
in Britain, the Romans built stadia for entertainment
and military training.

Wembley Stadium, London. Designed as part of a
major exhibition complex in 1924, it is now the nation's
largest forum for soccer and rock events.

Pittville Pump Room, Cheltenham, Gloucestershire.
An elegant example of 1820s Regency architecture, the
Pittville Pump Room is set in beautiful grounds. Its
gallery and dome surmount a great hall. Columns
surround the fountain which dispenses the waters.

Royal Pump Room, Harrogate, Yorkshire. The Royal
Pump Room supplied over 1,000 glasses of sulphur
water in a single morning during the height of its
popularity after opening in 1804.

1. The Globe Theatre, London. A reconstruction of the theatre is shown here. It was originally built in 1610, entirely of wood. When the landlord increased the ground rent, William Shakespeare and his fellow actors totally dismantled the building and rebuilt it on a new, cheaper site. The foundations of the Rose Theatre, a similar building, can be seen at Southwark, London.

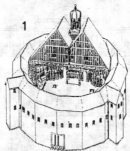

2. The Palace Theatre, London. New technology influences building development. The Palace Theatre was, in the 1890s, an early example of the use of electricity for ventilation and illumination. Architectural features simply became decorations to clad the new iron structure and cantilevered interior balconies.

3. Cinema, Rayners Lane, London. Concrete and glass, the former strong and able to be cast in any form, the latter light and thin, were both used extensively by the architects of the early 20th century. Cinemas in Britain, during the depression years between the two world wars, became dream palaces where people could yield to the magic of the screen.

The Pier and Palace, Brighton, Sussex. Known as the "first pier in the world", it was a splendid and exuberant cast-iron structure, now sadly gone as the former seaside trippers now holiday elsewhere, neglecting the bracing wind of the English Channel.

The Palace and Aquarium, Morecambe, Lancashire. On the north-west coast of England, it is a subtropical wonderland of plants, fish and Victorian extravagance.

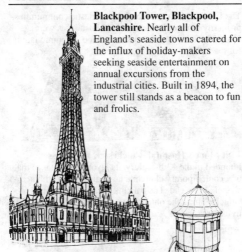

Blackpool Tower, Blackpool, Lancashire. Nearly all of England's seaside towns catered for the influx of holiday-makers seeking seaside entertainment on annual excursions from the industrial cities. Built in 1894, the tower still stands as a beacon to fun and frolics.

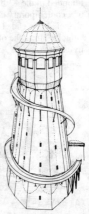

The Helter Skelter, Battersea Funfair, London. A wooden structure devised to be able to be dismantled and transported.

The first hospitals were built by monastic communities, primarily to care for the elderly. Almshouses were funded by local benefactors to provide accommodation for the aged.

1. St Mary's Hospital, Chichester, West Sussex.
Founded in the 13th century, its layout is similar to that of a contemporary church: a large aisled hall with a chapel at one end. The patients occupied beds or cubicles along the outer aisles. The central nave was the living area.

2. Browne's Hospital, Stamford, Lincolnshire. This beautiful building was financed by a gift from an Alderman Browne in 1490. The hospital, with its tall windows, takes up the central area of the hall beyond which lies the chapel. Through the door on the left there is a passage to a courtyard containing small residences for nurses and wardens.

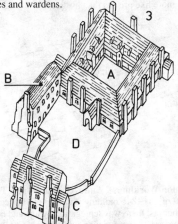

3. Almshouses and Grammar School, Ewelme, Oxfordshire. The aerial view of this group of early 15th-century buildings displays a configuration based upon a quadrangle. The hospital is housed within the quadrangle (**A**), outside is the master's house (**B**) and the school (**C**), with an enclosure for children (**D**).

The Inclosure Acts of the 18th century (which restricted the use of common land) and urban growth led to an increasing number of homeless people migrating from the countryside to the towns. By the mid-19th century, workhouses had been constructed on the outskirts of most cities to house the destitute. Such workhouses were more like prisons than hostels.

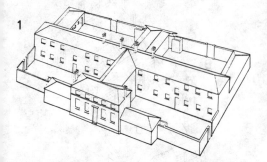

1. Union Workhouse, Andover, Hampshire. The layout of this 1846 building is typical of 19th-century workhouses: there was segregation by age and by sex, and meagre accommodation was offered in exchange only for hard labour. These gaunt buildings were made infamous in Dickens's *Oliver Twist*.

2. Arlington House, Camden Town, London. Even as late as 1901, when this was built, it was necessary to accommodate the poor or destitute. This hostel has cubicles for 1,150 men and is still in use.

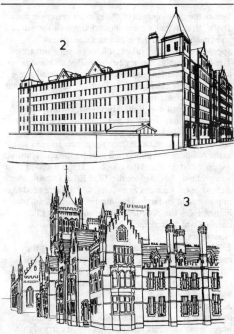

3. The Holloway Sanatorium, Virginia Water, Berkshire. Here, a 19th-century building, embellished with features in the Tudor and Gothic styles, was used to house the mentally and physically ill.

Before the development of the railway system in the 1840s, Britain had a great network of roads for wagons and coaches. In 1720, the coaches travelled at approximately 5 to 7 miles an hour on poor surfaces. The fastest public journey from London to Manchester took four-and-a-half days! Strategically located along all routes were coaching inns for food, accommodation, repairs and changing horses.

1. King's Head and Bell, Abingdon, Oxfordshire. A small inn which clearly shows the features of a town inn. The building is deep, with a tall, narrow front, and has no ordinary entrance from the street. To gain access to the building, the public had to enter the courtyard via the door that admitted the coaches. The low coach door was probably built before the 1755 Road Improvements Act extracted finances from tolls, which were used to improve road surfaces. The improvements meant that higher doors were needed in coaching inns for larger coaches which could now safely carry outside passengers.

2. The Bell, Stilton, Cambridgeshire. One of the regular stops on the old main road from London to Edinburgh, located 60 miles, or one day's drive, north of London. The steps outside the building were for mounting horses.

3. The King's Arms, Kendal, Cumbria. When this inn was built in the late 18th century, the road improvements meant that coaches could carry eight passengers inside and ten on the roof! The entrance is as high as the first-floor ceiling.

1

2

3

The New Inn, Gloucester, Gloucestershire. This view is from within the courtyard, looking towards the street. The stairs provide an entrance to a gallery. A door at the foot of the staircase leads to the food and beer hall, which gives access to rooms for the guests. At the back of the yard were stables and coach sheds.

The George, Southwark, London. Built in 1676, The George was one of over 25 inns in the same street that led directly from the bridge across the Thames to the road to Dover, from where passengers sailed for Europe. The galleries gave access to small rooms where guests would spend the night before an early morning start on their journey. Only one side of a quadrangle of balconies now remains.

St Pancras Station Hotel, London. Sir George Gilbert
Scott built St Pancras Station Hotel of coloured brick so
that it would stand out in the smog. During the 1860s
and 1870s there was a boom of hotel building in
London to cater for an increasingly mobile international
and imperial society. Some of the earliest and largest
hotels were built adjacent to London's railway termini.
Built between 1868 and 1874, this hotel (formerly the
Midland Grand Hotel, and today used for offices) was,
with 400 beds, the largest hotel of its time.

The construction of these huge hotels was facilitated by
the invention of the hydraulic lift in 1857.

1. The Albion Hotel, Broadstairs, Kent. A purpose-built seaside hotel opened in 1816 and still in use. It is typical of seaside accommodation: it faces the sea; it has a first-floor viewing gallery; and, originally, it had a ground floor terrace – which is now glazed and forms a comfortable veranda on which to sit and watch seaside activities.

2. Grand Hotel, Scarborough, Yorkshire. Built in 1863, and made possible by the railway system which brought the new, affluent middle classes to the Yorkshire seaside resort. These Victorian palaces housed ball rooms, games rooms and terraces for viewing the seascape.

1. Coffee House, Exeter, Devon. An Elizabethan meeting house for sea captains for the purpose of obtaining trade and crew.

2. Public House, Bury St Edmunds, Suffolk. A contender for being the smallest pub in England. Public houses of whatever size have become the focus for community gatherings and a unique feature of the British way of life.

3. Cricket Pavilion, Oxford, Oxfordshire. It contains a clock, a veranda under which players can shelter, and timber decoration reminiscent of Tudor buildings.

4. Club, "Boodle's", London. A gentlemen's town club, built in 1775 and decorated with an elegant facade for the exclusive membership. The club is still used by members for bridge and gossip.

5. Golf Club, Royal and Ancient, St Andrews, Fife.
This building displays the typical features of a sports
clubhouse: large windows and terraces from which the
members may view the greens.

5. Agricultural buildings

The early farm, even during Roman times, housed the farmer's family, workers, the livestock and winter fodder.

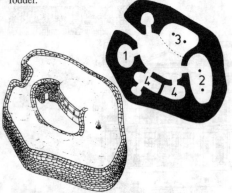

Chysaster, Cornwall. An early Iron Age farmstead probably housing two families (**1, 2**). These rooms and the livestock (**3**) and storage rooms (**4**) were grouped around a central open courtyard. Access to the farm complex was via a narrow and low doorway. The construction would be of undressed stone with a turf roof.

None of the pre-Roman farms have survived, and reconstructions are based upon archaeological evidence and conjecture.

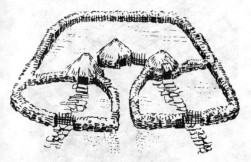

Romano-British Farm, Riding Wood, Northumberland. This is a drawing of a model of the farm. Cattle or sheep would have been penned within the secure enclosures.

Petersfield, Hampshire. A wood and thatch structure built recently as an example of an Iron Age farm building. A circular central hall is surrounded by stalls for cattle and storerooms for forage. It would have had a stockade to protect the livestock from forest predators.

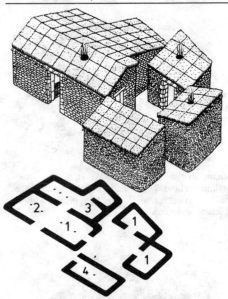

Mawgan Porth, Cornwall. The Saxons built rough stone buildings in which farmers lived alongside their livestock. This farm had three living quarters (**1**), byres for cattle (**2**), a fodder store (**3**) and additional rooms for tools (**4**). All the buildings would have been closely built to give narrow and difficult entrances for possible intruders.

Makenfield Hall, Ripon, Yorkshire. The above drawing is of the medieval moated farm complex of a very prosperous farmer. Although the manor house is pre-1300, most of the outbuildings were added after the dissolution of the monasteries in the 1530s.

The drawing below is of the same farm in the mid-19th century. New and expansive cattlesheds were built among buildings which housed more modern agricultural implements.

Longhouse, Llanerfyl, Powys. Early dry-stone farmhouses had one long range of rooms with a common roof. Each half would have been divided by a central cross passage (**1**). The farmer's living quarters would have been at one end (**2**) and the livestock kept at the other end (**3**). The two additional doors on the drawing above were added later.

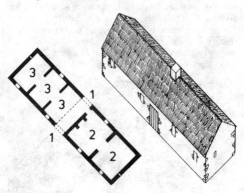

Bastel House. The Yorkshire and north-west region of England had farmhouses in which the residence (**1**) was above the livestock and storage space (**2**). These houses were particularly common during the period of the moorland enclosures in the early 19th century.

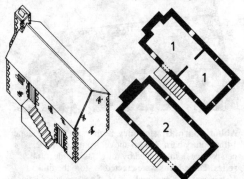

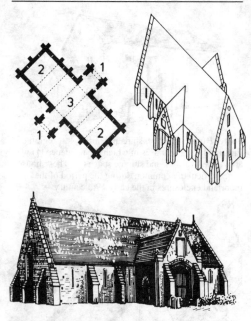

Abbot's Barn, Glastonbury, Somerset. A large stone 14th-century barn (shown above, from various perspectives), influenced by religious architectural styles. These barns were erected to store the tithe (a 10 per cent tax) paid by tenants of ecclesiastical lands.

Activities within large barns had been carried out in the same manner for over 1,000 years. High-loaded wagons entered the barn at (**1**) (hence the high doors), and the sheaves were stored at the two ends (**2**). During the winter months the corn was threshed in the middlestead (**3**), either on a hard, earth floor, or on a raised platform. After the threshing, the large doors at either side were opened, and the corn was winnowed by allowing the through draught to separate the chaff and straw from the corn.

Well Covering. Re-erected in the Weald and Downland Open Air Museum, Chichester, West Sussex. This is a fine example of a medieval well-house, from which a farm's supply of water could be drawn.

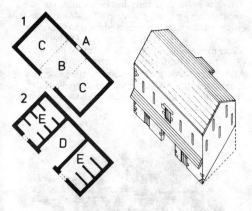

Bank Barn. These barns were built in hilly regions. They had the advantage that access could be gained to the upper floor (**1**) by a door (**A**) set in the opposite side, higher up the hill. The central area of the upper floor (**B**) was used for threshing, and the two bays (**C**) for storage. The lower storey (**2**) usually had a central area (**D**) for carts, with side bays (**E**) for cattle and horses.

Cressing Temple, Essex. A vast wooden-structured medieval barn.

Dutch Barn. These barns provide basic cover for storage. Usually constructed on a concrete base for dryness, they feature metal supports and metal sheet roofing.

Silo. Recent farm landscapes feature tubular prefabricated silage or grain stores. They are usually made of pre-cast sheets of concrete or steel panels.

The most hated landmark of a medieval farm was the dovecote. In medieval times the local peasants were not permitted to keep or kill pigeons, which were kept exclusively by the landowners for provision of winter meat. Most housed between 500 and 1,000 birds which were free to rob the local farms of their seed or crops. By the 18th century, when everyone was permitted to keep pigeons, a survey revealed that there were 26,000 dovecotes in Britain.

1. Dovecote, Daylingworth, Gloucestershire. An example of a circular medieval dovecote.
2. Dovecote, Chastleton, Oxfordshire. A 17th-century rectangular building.

Granary, Cowdray, Sussex. Timber box-frame and brick set on mushroom-shaped stones. These footings were devised to deter rats and other rodents.

Granary, Bramley, Surrey. A tiled store set on brick columns, under which carts could be stored.

The 18th and 19th centuries saw a great change in farming practices. Metal field machines, reapers, sowers, ploughs, threshers, rollers, hoers – all of these required storage. The horses needed stables, and the new agricultural and horticultural techniques resulted in increased livestock populations, also all requiring stabling. Intensive farming of pigs, cows and hens, and the introduction of winter fodder and new farm implements meant that farms became, for the first time, industrial units whose layout was intended for maximum efficiency and profitability.

Stables, Cart and Cattle Sheds, Painsthorpe, Yorkshire. It became common practice to set rows of accommodation – preferably on a slight slope for the sewage to drain away – around a central courtyard.
1. Cart sheds.
2. Stables to house draught horses.
3. Barn for horses' fodder, with further cart sheds beneath.

Stables, Crewe, Cheshire. Every farm had its row of stables, with accommodation for a groom, and haylofts above.

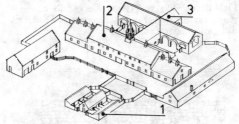

Tattenhall Farm, Cheshire. A mid-19th century design for a farm complex. The buildings were grouped to form yards, in which the cattle herds could be fed to fatten them up before slaughter. The pigs were no longer free range but were kept in pens and sheds (**1**), and the central complex (**2**) could house a steam-driven threshing machine. Large sheds were provided for the field machinery (**3**).

Field Barns. Often built on the sides of hills for protection from winter storms, these exposed buildings had small windows and doors.

Field House. The Lake District and Pennine slopes contain two-storey, dry-stone buildings which were used to house young cattle on the lower floor. The upper floor was for winter feed for sheep, which were kept in pens alongside.

Cattle Pound, Yorkshire. Small corrals of stone, to provide winter and spring shelter for free-range sheep or cattle.

Outhouse, Connemara, Galway, Ireland. The exposed Atlantic coasts of Ireland, Scotland and the south west of England have many small, dry-stone circular buildings often with turf or thatched roofs. These are used for pigs or as hen houses, or to keep fuel dry.

Barn and Shelter, Deptford, Wiltshire. The design of these remote storage buildings has remained unchanged for over 1,500 years. The one above has clay walls covered in thatch for protection. It has a barn, cattle byres and a small store.

There were two sorts of watermill: the undershot, in which water passed under the wheel; and the overshot in which it passed over. The undershot was the most common, as overshot watermills required a flow of water from an elevation above the height of the wheel, best found in steep valleys where water has a good downward force.

1

1. Corn Mill, Wrexham, Clwyd. A timber-framed building erected in 1661, with a large 16-foot diameter undershot wheel mounted outside the building.

2. Malt Distilling Mill, Bromley-by-Bow, Essex. Built with a timber-framed structure; by its completion in 1776 brick was available to encase the facade. It has four undershot water wheels.

3. Grain Mill, Horstead, Norfolk. Built only 20 years later, in 1789, it too strides across the river and uses undershot wheels. The cabins protruding from the top floor, called locums, housed winding gear used to raise the grain from boats moored below to the upper stories of the mill.

2

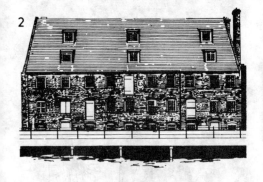

3

1. Windmill, Cley, Norfolk. This mill stays stationary and only the top cap revolves to face the wind.
2. Post Mill, Whittlesford, Cambridgeshire. This early 19th-century windmill is called a post mill. The extended tail fan turns the mill, which is supported on a central post, into the oncoming wind. English windmill building was developed primarily as a result of Dutch engineering skills that were learnt during the draining of the East Anglian fens in the 18th century.

Gin House, Howden, Yorkshire. Before power from steam or petrol engines was introduced, farm machines were driven by a horse or horses circulating around a treadmill in a horse engine house. This Yorkshire one originally had open sides which have subsequently been boarded up. The diagram shows the revolving wheel which is connected by a shaft called a "gin" to the threshing machine which would be located in the barn.

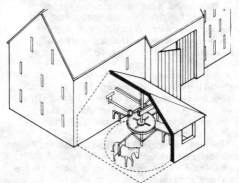

1, 2. Oast-house, Kent. Amid the acres of apple orchards and hop fields of south-east England, oast-houses strike a characteristic silhouette. Consisting of brick ovens and timber buildings, they are small agricultural factories for drying the August crop of hops.

The cylindrical ovens (**A**) blow hot air up through layers of hops (**B**) and out through the vents (**C**). After drying, the hops are laid out on the upper floor (**D**) to cool, and are then pressed (**E**) into large sacks (**F**), which are lowered to the ground floor (**G**) to await delivery to the brewery.

3. Maltings, Snape, Suffolk. Although retaining the traditional roof structure of a 19th-century malting works for the drying and processing of barley, it is now converted into a concert hall.

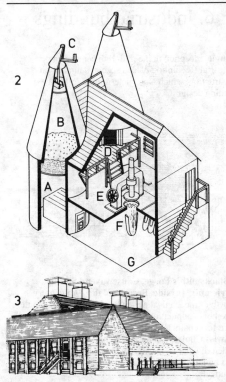

6. Industrial buildings

From its inception in the mid-18th century, the
Industrial Revolution placed special demands on
construction, which had a determining influence on
building design.

**1. Blacksmith's Forge, Causewayend Smithy,
Kirriemuir, Tayside.** Because of the 19th-century
growth of mechanical agricultural implements and the
large horse population, every rural community had a
forge for repairs to metalwork.
2. Swiss Chalet, Rochester, Kent. Originally in the
garden of Charles Dickens at Gad's Hill, Kent, it was
used by Dickens as a retreat in which he wrote some of
his novels.

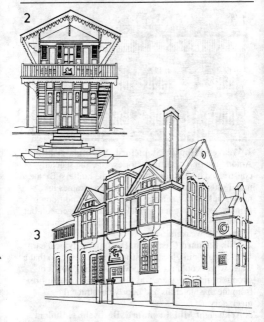

3. Studio House, Kensington, London. Prosperous Victorian painters could commission architects to build private studios to their own needs. This grand house has vast windows on the first floor which illuminate the artist's studio.

1. Weavers' Houses, Stapleford, Nottinghamshire.
Among the first types of factories were the specially
constructed houses for stocking-frame knitters. By the
mid-1840s, there were 16,000 weavers' frames in
homes in Nottinghamshire alone. The ground floor and
front were laid out in a normal terrace arrangement, but
the top floor had large windows to allow maximum
light on the weavers' work.

2. Mill, Barnard Castle, Co. Durham. A typical early
19th-century mill, located astride a small river, so that a
water wheel could produce power. Although built of
strong local stone, there was always a high risk of fire
from the dry materials and poorly constructed
machinery.

3. Arkwright Mill, Cromford, Derbyshire. Built in
1785, the design was based on a military idea. The
ground floor had a tiny entrance and strong gateway,
devised to make the factory impenetrable to rioting
handloom weavers, whose work had been replaced by
machine looms.

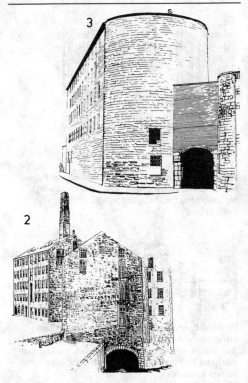

Piano Factory, Camden Town, London. By the mid-18th century, factories of all types were being erected. The Industrial Revolution created new demands, requiring innovative design. This circular building, constructed in the 1860s, offers maximum light for the workers on every floor.

Flour Mill, Swansea, West Glamorgan. Britain's earliest reinforced concrete building, erected in 1897. An example of the box-like construction method that was to replace traditional brick, stone and even iron-framed structures.

Coty Factory, Great West Road, Heston, Greater London. On the edges of cities, where land values were lower, and communications had, by the 1930s, greatly improved, palaces of industry were built. The facades were decorated with a confidence that reflected the belief that the future would bring a bright new world for the workers and capitalist financiers.

Boots Factory, Beeston, Nottinghamshire. Function here dictates form. This is a large structure of reinforced concrete columns and floors, with wide expanses of glass walls and roofs. The 1930 factory was the result of the new design ideas imported from the German Bauhaus school of architecture.

1. North Staffordshire Potteries Museum, Stoke-on-Trent, Staffordshire. The form of industrial buildings is primarily governed by their function: the bottle kilns, typical of coal-fed potteries and larger forms of glass manufacture, are an excellent example of this principle. The kilns would be filled with a pyramid of pots, which would be evenly fired by the heat of the coal fires reflected down from the walls.

2. Walls Ice Cream Factory, Acton, London, 1930s.

3. Clyde Foundry, Govan, Glasgow, Strathclyde, 1920. The foundry and ice cream factory, although of different sizes and functions, are similarly built. They are both constructed using structural steel-box framing, which is cheap and does not require internal walls, which would divide up the large floor area that any factory needs. The use of glass roofs allows natural light to reach the whole work area.

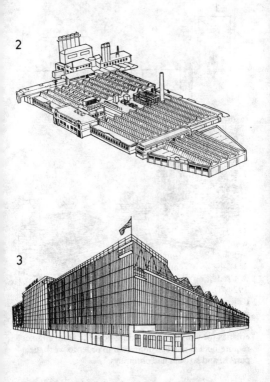

2

3

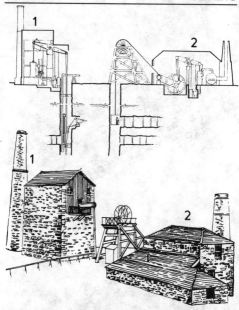

Copper Mine, Levant, Cornwall. This mid-19th-century mine has a high-pressure beam engine in the pumping house (**1**). The lower building houses the engines for working the winding gear (**2**). Both engines require boilers and consume coal in order to work the pumps, and so both had chimneys.

The Industrial Revolution of the last century required vast quantities of fuel and raw materials like copper, lead and iron ore. Mines usually had two main buildings: the pumping house (**1**) to remove water from below ground; and the winding house (**2**) to raise and lower the workers and minerals.

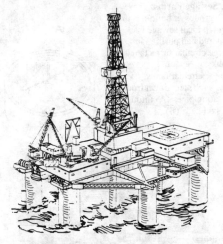

Shell Ocean Voyager Oil Exploration Rig. The later half of the 20th century heralded the discovery and exploitation of North Sea oil and gas, which resulted in huge structures, such as this 1970's rig, being erected far off the north-east coast of Britain.

Water for public consumption in towns is usually drawn from wells and pumped to the top of a tall tower to maintain pressure in delivery pipes. Water-pumping stations tend to have an obtrusive appearance. Being difficult to disguise, architects have used imaginative ideas to render them more congenial.

1. Sewage Farms. These are groups of buildings in which local sewage is filtered and purified in large circular or rectangular tanks.

In the circular tanks, sewage filters down from rotating pipes (**A**) through gravel beds (**B**).

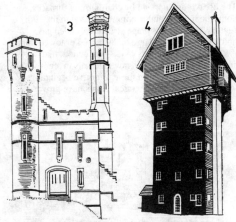

2. Abbey Mills Pumping Station, London. A Byzantine-style building erected in 1865 to house vast beam engines; used to raise the level of the outflow of sewage in a low-lying, flat area in east London.

3. Waterworks Pumping Station, Manor House, London. A turreted and castle-keep arrangement of the pumping house and raised water tank.

4. The House in the Clouds, Thorpeness, Suffolk. Built in 1923 to supply water to a seaside holiday resort, this water tower has been disguised as a house on a tower. The top section has imitation windows and chimney, but the lower floors contain real living accommodation.

The use of gas, supplied by coal-burning furnaces, for domestic lighting and heating, increased in the 19th century. It required storage structures, called gas holders, which were large tanks, raised or lowered into the ground. By-products of gas production, like coke and coal tar, were used as raw materials in a growing chemical industry. From these primitive beginnings today's sophisticated chemical plants have grown.

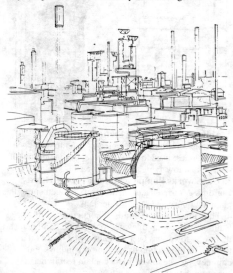

Ellesmere Port, Cheshire. An oil refinery is a baffling maze of pipes and structures. The sequence of stages needed to purify crude oil and extract by-products requires large expanses of land, usually located on the coast, to provide access for oil tankers bringing imported oil, or to connect pipes from off-shore oil, direct to the refinery.

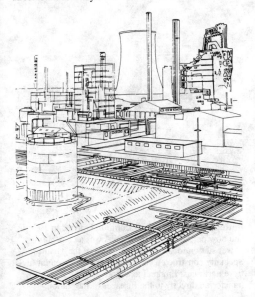

Energy requirements in the 20th century have become a major environmental issue. New environmentally friendly energy sources, such as solar, tidal, wind, hydro or thermal power, have been poorly exploited. Traditional methods of coal burning to power electrical generators, or the use of nuclear reactors, are now considered potential hazards to the environment.

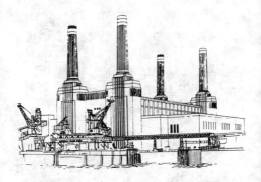

Battersea Power Station, London. Opened in 1934, and now partially dismantled, this was a coal-burning power station located near the banks of the Thames. Specially constructed coastal collier boats brought fuel from north-east England to a quay where it was transferred directly to the furnaces of the station.

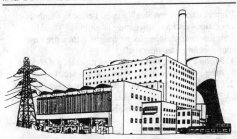

Ferrybridge Power Station, Yorkshire. Huge cooling towers constantly discharge steam, and the coal-burning furnaces require large and frequent loads of coal to be brought from the nearby Yorkshire coalfields.

Atomic Reactor, Dounreay, Highland. Built in 1959 and located on Scotland's northern coastline, this was the world's first fast reactor, which for 18 years regularly produced electricity. Grave doubts now exist about the wisdom of the use of atomic fuels, most notably because of their possible adverse effects on future environmental conditions.

Lighthouses are invaluable in bad coastal weather conditions and for navigating at night.

Originally containing living quarters, they are now mainly computer-operated.

1. Stone Pharos, Dover, Kent. An octagonal Roman lighthouse built to guide ships coming from France.

2. Lighthouse, Burnham-on-Sea, Somerset. Built in the 18th century to warn against inshore sandbanks.

3. Lighthouse, Dungeness, Kent. A 20th-century structure built to replace the previous lighthouse, which is now too far inland due to coastal growth.

4. Eddystone Lighthouse, off Plymouth, Devon. The most famous British lighthouse. Built by John Smeaton in 1759, its stone structure has withstood many storms. Its main structure is assembled from interlocking stones (**A**) creating a strong base (**B**), above which there are storage rooms (**C**) and living quarters (**D**) all set below the light room (**E**).

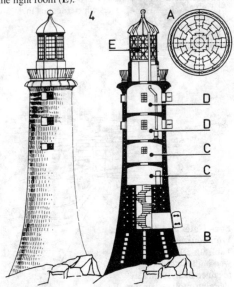

Toll House, Littleborough, Nottinghamshire. The 1750's toll acts provided for the repair and upkeep of the nation's roads. Keepers' houses were placed at intervals and featured toll gates which blocked the road.

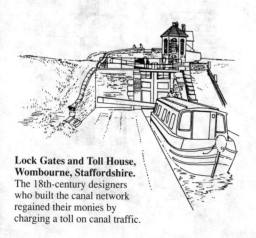

Lock Gates and Toll House, Wombourne, Staffordshire. The 18th-century designers who built the canal network regained their monies by charging a toll on canal traffic.

Motel, Ilfracombe, Devon. The American idea of a complex of individual overnight accommodation has been adopted on the major motorways and at some seaside resorts.

Bus Stations. Twentieth-century public transport systems have produced vast changes of styles for both the public bus stations and garages.

The railway age covered the British Isles, especially between the years 1830 to 1870, with a network of interconnecting routes that were accompanied by innumerable specialized buildings. Built for the needs of the public and of commerce, as well as for the railways' own requirements, most of these buildings are now forgotten and derelict, or have been demolished after lines have ceased to be used or technological advance has rendered them superfluous.

1. Charlbury Station, Oxfordshire. Built in 1853, this is a small stopping-station typical of hundreds that were to follow. It featured a large overhanging roof on the front and back to protect waiting passengers, toilets at the end wall and a central chimney for the waiting-room fireplace. The seats and the weatherboard cladding affixed to a wooden structure all became standard features of railway-station architecture.
2. Footbridge, Wilmcote, Warwickshire. An 1880's decorated pedestrian rail crossing, made of cast-iron parts.

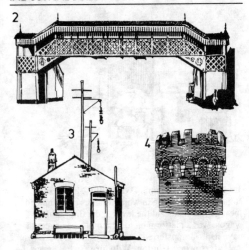

3. Weighbridge, Lambeth, London. By the 1880s, railways were the major freight handlers, and many stations had a weighbridge house, where vehicles were weighed, both empty and full, to determine the cargoes' weight.

4. Ventilator, Chipping Sodbury, Avon. This is not a miniature castle: it is the air vent from a tunnel on the Great Western Railway from London to Bristol. An engineering genius, Isambard Kingdom Brunel, devised ways to tunnel under the Duke of Beaufort's estates and thus spare the gentleman's sensibility.

1. Goods Shed, Thame, Oxfordshire. Every small station had a building in which wagons could unload local goods. Inside, at the level of the floor of the wagon, was a platform on to which the wagon could have its load transferred.

2. Watertower, Swindon, Wiltshire. Swindon was the nerve centre of the Great Western Railway. Until the 1960s, when diesel and electric trains became more economical, steam trains needed to replenish their boilers with water. These towers were a familiar sight on "water sidings" of all railway systems.

3. Signal Box, Pewsey, Wiltshire. Transferring a train from one track to another was done manually by levers located in a signal box. Before the introduction of the telephone or radio, each box was linked to the others and to the stations by telegraph, which alerted the controllers to the direction and timings of rail traffic.

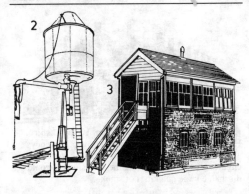

4. The Roundhouse, Camden Town, London. Robert Stephenson, brother of George, designed this circular engine shed in 1846. Railway engineers constructed buildings throughout the country which served functional needs and had few stylistic features.

Engine Sheds, Stratford-on-Avon, Warwickshire.
Home for tired engines. Notice the row of chimneys
along both sides of the roof, here because steam
engines, even when entering the shed slowly, would
discharge large quantities of smoke.

Level Crossing House, Upton Lovell, Wiltshire.
Each road/railway crossing was controlled by an on-site
resident, a "crossing keeper". Trains could come down
the line at any time of the day or night, so a constant
vigil was required.

King's Cross, London. The south terminal of the Great Northern Railway. A wonderful simple structure of the 1850s which has suffered subsequent modern additions.

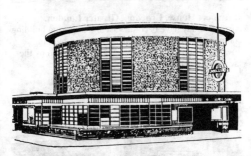

Underground Station, Arnos Grove, London. An architect's geometrical solution to the problem of providing an underground station with a separate public entrance and exit, built in 1932.

1. Airport House, Croydon, Greater London.
Airports today have become vast and imposing building complexes. The first ever British terminal building, however, is much less intrusive, as exemplified by the facade shown above.

2. Terminal 4, Heathrow Airport, Greater London.
This large terminal can serve up to 22 aircraft
simultaneously, 17 of which could be jumbo jets.
Designed to be "passenger friendly", there is only a
short distance – all on one level – between the
terminal's car park or underground station and the
aircraft. By segregating arriving and departing
passengers, the architects have also succeeded in giving
departing passengers access to restaurants and shops.
3. Stansted Airport, Essex. Opened in March 1991, it
is designed to accommodate eight million passengers
every year. The building is constructed out of thin metal
frames which support both glass walls and roof
coverings.

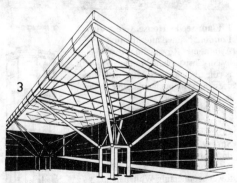

3

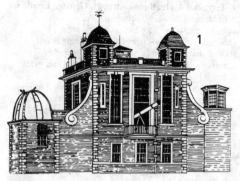

1. Flamsteed's House, Greenwich, London. Named after the first Astronomer Royal, and probably built by Sir Christopher Wren in 1675–6, it is constructed of red brick with stone dressing. The octagonal upper room houses telescopes.

It was established as the Royal Observatory in the 18th century.

2. Semaphore Tower, Cobham, Surrey. In anticipation of invasion during the Napoleonic Wars, the Admiralty built a series of semaphore towers connecting Whitehall and Portsmouth.

3. Radio Telescope, Jodrell Bank, Cheshire. Built in 1957 to observe the invisible outerspace phenomena detected by radio waves.

4. Post Office Tower, London. Built in 1966 with the prime intention of relaying signals to regions beyond London. As radio transmissions travel in straight lines it was necessary, in the days before satellites could "bounce" waves back over obstacles, to elevate the transmitters or receivers to overcome the earth's curvature and other obstructions.

7. Monuments and follies

Chamber Tomb, Maeshowe, Orkney. The earliest monument builders were neolithic tomb builders using a dry-stone corbelled technique similar to the early eastern Mediterranean builders. After the construction of tunnels and the domed tomb (**1**) the entire building was encased in a mound of earth (**2**). Those on the Orkneys are the finest in the British Isles.

Lanyan Quoit, Cornwall. From the Orkneys in the farthest north of Scotland to Cornwall in the south west of England, the remains of neolithic stone long barrows survive in different forms. The erosion of the encasing earth, which left only the interior stone structure as evidence for their use, provides a somewhat limited basis from which many interpretations of their function have been made. In Scotland and Ireland such a standing stone group is called a "dolmen", in Wales a "cromlech". All are now believed to be burial mounds.

Highgate Cemetery, London. Featuring the Lebanon Circle catacombs and small private chambers built into the side of a steep hill, containing, in lead and metal coffins, the remains of London Victorian society.
In the early 19th century, urban growth inflated the already increasing population growth, which meant that churchyard burial grounds were overflowing. The parliamentary sanitary reform of 1820 heralded the building of commercial cemeteries, many of whose monumental splendours survive as memorials to the occupants.

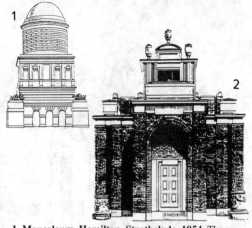

1. Mausoleum, Hamilton, Strathclyde, 1854. The
mausoleum of Alexander, 10th Duke of Hamilton,
dominates the surrounding landscape. Inside, the Duke
lies in a black marble sarcophagus which once held the
remains of an ancient Egyptian Pharaoh.

2. Mausoleum, Dulwich, London. In 1814 the
architect Sir John Soane and the deceased Sir Francis
Bourgeois left a fitting memorial to their skills and
intelligence. Soane devised a mausoleum, paid for by
Bourgeois' estate, whose main building was an art
gallery containing a collection of paintings, primarily
by Dutch masters, bequeathed by Sir Francis to the
local school.

Bonomi Pyramid, Blickling Hall, Norfolk. A 40-foot-high repository for the remains of the 2nd Earl of Buckingham and his two wives. A 19th-century Pharaoh's tomb for English country gentlefolk.

Crematorium, Golders Green, London. Nowadays every city and town has a crematorium, but in the 1860s Sir Henry Thompson had to apply political agitation to establish the secular Cremation Society. Golders Green (1905) is an early example of the factory for departing souls.

1. Cupid's Column, Plymouth, Devon. This 18th-century obelisk once stood in the grounds of Mount Edgcumbe, but was later moved to a hill overlooking Plymouth Sound. It was erected by a Countess in memory of her pig, Cupid.

2. Albert Memorial, Kensington, London. Queen Victoria's memorial to her husband Prince Albert, completed in 1876, 16 years after his death. A 19th-century storybook of representations of Europe, America, Africa and Asia. Designed by Gilbert Scott, it contains 169 life-size figures of famous painters, architects, musicians, poets and sculptors, and features groups of figures representing Faith, Hope, Charity and Humility, and statues symbolizing agriculture, manufacturing, commerce and engineering.

3. The Monument, London. This was built to
commemorate the 1666 Great Fire of London. When
erected 10 years later, London had, under the architect
Sir Christopher Wren, risen from the ashes with new
wide streets, elegant brick or stone buildings, 51 new
churches, and the new St Paul's Cathedral was under
construction.

4. Penshaw Monument, Sunderland, Tyne and Wear.
Dark, dirty Doric columns erected in 1842 by a public
subscription from the local inhabitants in north-east
England. Visible for miles, it was originally intended as
a memorial to John George Lambton, 1st Earl Of
Durham.

1. The Gosforth Cross, Gosforth, Cumbria. A mixture of Christian symbols and Celtic cross and circle, with depictions of Nordic legends. These "wheel" crosses mostly occur in regions occupied by the Scandinavian invaders in the 5th century. Many are to be found in northern England, Ireland, Wales, the Isle of Man and south-west Scotland.

Devoted medieval Christians erected elaborate crosses or small columned structures culminating in a cross as evidence of private or communal glorification of God, or of the memory of a loved one. The most famous in England were the series of crosses erected by Edward I in 1291 on sites where his wife Eleanor's body was laid to rest on the journey from Harby, Nottinghamshire, to London.

2. Weeping Stone, Ampney Crucis, Cirencester, Gloucestershire. Christians believe in penitence and the forgiveness of sinners. Crosses and tall stones were often used as a focal point from which churchmen on a pilgrimage could pray for God's forgiveness.

3. The Market Cross, Chichester, West Sussex. Built and donated to the town by Bishop Edward Story in 1501.

4. The Poultry Cross, Salisbury, Wiltshire. A 14th-century market cross that was originally the centre of poultry sales.

5. The Market Cross, Malmesbury, Wiltshire. Built in the 13th century and still surviving as a local gathering place for shoppers.

Arches were often built with Roman military ideals in mind. They were intended to impress the patrons' power and success upon the person passing through the arch. The nation's capital also has numerous arches constructed to commemorate monarchs and victories.

1. Norman Gate, Bury St Edmunds, Suffolk. Built in 1120 at the height of Norman power. The Benedictine abbey was one of the wealthiest and most important in the country.

2. York Water Gate, London. Set close to the banks of the River Thames, it was built in 1626. The gate was the quayside entrance to York House, the residence of the Duke of Buckingham. The house no longer exists, and the Thames embankment has pushed the water back 100 yards, so now the gateway stands alone in a small park.

3. Marble Arch, London. Designed by John Nash in 1818 and built a mile from the forecourt of Buckingham Palace as the special entrance for George IV and his family. It was moved in 1851 to the north-east corner of Hyde Park, opposite Speakers' Corner. The present site of the arch was, from the end of the 15th century to 1783, the site of the Tyburn Tree, where London's public executions took place.

1

2

3

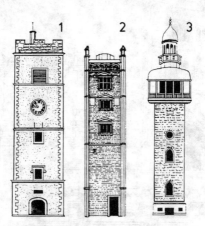

Towers have an appeal because of their distinctiveness. Standing alone, they display the flair of their creators.

1. Clock Tower, St Albans, Hertfordshire. Built in the 15th century as a curfew tower.

2. Freston Tower, Ipswich, Suffolk. A 16th-century folly built by Lord Freston on the banks of the River Orwell.

3. Carillon Tower, Loughborough, Leicestershire. This is really a memorial to the First World War.

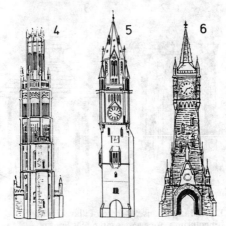

4. May's Folly, Hadlow, Kent. Built in 1840 it stands 170 feet high.

5. Abberley Clock Tower, Worcester, Hereford and Worcester. Built in 1883 by John Jones to house 20 bells which can play 40 different tunes.

6. Machynlleth's Clock Tower, Machynlleth, Powys. A gift to the town by the Marquis of Londonderry, a local landowner.

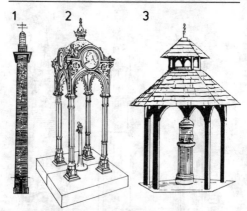

1. Land Lighthouse, Dunston Pillar, Lincoln, Lincolnshire. A generous gift by Sir Francis Dashwood, who in 1751 had erected a tower to help guide travellers across the featureless heathland south of Lincoln. From 1809 it had a statue of George III on the top. It was reduced to a stump in 1940 as it was endangering a local airfield.

2. Drinking Fountain, Greenock, Strathclyde. Many towns have public drinking fountains featuring these cast iron covers. They were erected in 1897 to commemorate Queen Victoria's Diamond Jubilee.

3. Village pump, Westmill, Hertfordshire. Before the advent of indoor plumbing, water for drinking and washing was only available from a communal well.

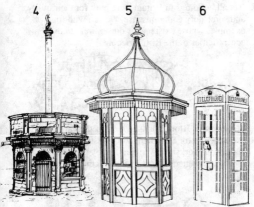

4. Mercat Cross, Prestonpass, East Lothian. A
symbol of municipal authority in prosperous Scottish
burghs. They were used as a platform for proclamations
and as a gathering point for the weekly market or
seasonal fair.

5. Kiosk, Bangor Pier, Gwynedd. A 19th-century
extravaganza in entertainment architecture. The toll
entrance to a pier.

6. British Telephone Kiosk. Due to vandalism and
commercial philistinism, the traditional red box will no
longer be a feature on the British landscape.

Not all buildings in Britain were built for their utility, and some defy commonsense. We end with four examples whose existence is due entirely to the eccentricities of the British people.

Stonehenge, Ilton, Yorkshire. As if the variety of explanations for Stonehenge in Wiltshire were not enough, in Yorkshire, William Danby provided work for the local unemployed in constructing a replica stone circle.

Tattingstone Wonder, Tattingstone, Suffolk. An 18th-century country gentleman wished to have a distant view of a village church from his window. This building is actually a house – note the chimney on the roof.

McCraig's Tower, Oban, Strathclyde. Not the Colosseum, Rome, but an incomplete art gallery and museum constructed in the 1890s.

Twizel Castle, near Berwick-on-Tweed, Northumberland. A medieval fortress, built for Sir Francis Blake in 1770. It took 50 years to create an impression of a 1,000-year-old castle.

Index